"One of the greatest dangers for modern Christians is not apostasy but apathy. In the church, there are not masses of people who are in danger of denying Jesus, but some are in danger of growing bored with him. In *Overcoming Apathy*, we are met with practical ways for the church to fight back against one of our greatest challenges and we are confronted with the beauty of the gospel and the glory of King Jesus."

J. T. English, Lead Pastor, Storyline Fellowship, Arvada, Colorado; author, *Deep Discipleship*

"Uche Anizor speaks from his experience, encouraging us to recognize and resist apathy, which is so common in our day. Human apathy refers not to healthy rest or godly contentment, but the loss of motivation and the growth of indifference; this condition then often undermines love for God and neighbor. If you feel apathetic, have lost motivation, and wonder if God has anything to say about your indifference, let Anizor point you back toward our good God and his good purposes. You'll see that there is much worth living for because you have been liberated to care about things God cares about."

Kelly Kapic, Professor of Theological Studies, Covenant College; author, *You're Only Human*

"*Overcoming Apathy* is an honest invitation to take a tour of our hearts, where apathy often lives. Apathy, which has always been pervasive in fallen hearts, has been popularized by our present age to the point where we don't even notice its presence and power in our lives. Uche Anizor helps us identify and define apathy, disentangling it from other emotions and experiences. With nuance and relevance, he offers seven seed buds from which apathy grows, pairing each with an antidote from Scripture. He moves from philosophical discussion to practical suggestions with ease, offering hope to those who struggle with indifference to that which should most ignite us to love and adoration."

Aimee Joseph, author, *Demystifying Decision-Making*

"Uche Anizor has put his finger on one of the most disturbing and poignant cultural problems in the modern West: *apathy*. His psychologically insightful, theologically careful, and devotionally rich treatment will help readers both understand and overcome this 'sickness of the soul.' Both individual readers and small groups will benefit from Uche's wise diagnosis of the causes and nature of apathy, as well as from his discussion of how we find healing and escape from apathy in the gospel."

Gavin Ortlund, Senior Pastor, First Baptist Church of Ojai, California; author, *Finding the Right Hills to Die On*

Overcoming Apathy

Overcoming Apathy

Gospel Hope for Those Who Struggle to Care

Uche Anizor

WHEATON, ILLINOIS

Library of Congress Cataloging-in-Publication Data

Names: Anizor, Uche, 1976- author.
Title: Overcoming apathy : gospel hope for those who struggle to care / Uche Anizor.
Description: Wheaton, Illinois : Crossway, 2022. | Includes bibliographical references and index.
Identifiers: LCCN 2021019520 (print) | LCCN 2021019521 (ebook) | ISBN 9781433578809 (trade paperback) | ISBN 9781433578816 (pdf) | ISBN 9781433578823 (mobi) | ISBN 9781433578830 (epub)
Subjects: LCSH: Caring—Religious aspects—Christianity. | Apathy—Religious aspects—Christianity.
Classification: LCC BV4647.S9 A55 2022 (print) | LCC BV4647.S9 (ebook) | DDC 241/.3—dc23
LC record available at https://lccn.loc.gov/2021019520
LC ebook record available at https://lccn.loc.gov/2021019521

To John Piper,
whose ministry definitively shaped my desire
to fight for God-centered zeal
and against spiritual apathy

Contents

Preface

Something for the Strugglers

THIS BOOK IS AN EXPLORATION of apathy. My main concern is spiritual apathy, or indifference toward the core things that Christians should care about. These few chapters are my modest attempt to understand and address an experience so commonplace that it feels like an expected part of life.

I've been meaning to write this book for years as a way of understanding myself and the ups and downs of my own Christian life. I am not a psychologist, but I am someone who by experience, sadly, is intimately acquainted with the topic. I write as one Christian man to fellow travelers who are perplexed by their indifference to the things of God.

This book is not for those unwilling to change. It is for the perturbed, the struggling. It is for those who feel stuck, but want to change. It is for those who find their coldness mystifying *and* disturbing. It is for those who want to be passionate about the things of God but can't seem to care enough. I write for those who pray, "Lord, I care, but help my lack of caring!" This book is for true strugglers.

I don't intend this to be the definitive word on apathy. If you like to categorize books, this one should perhaps be placed in the category of practical or pastoral theology. As a theologian, I firmly believe that good theology is always done in conversation: primarily with Scripture, but also with other theologians and thinkers. I approach this topic similarly. Throughout these pages, we'll dialogue with pastors, monks, psychologists, theologians, philosophers, sociologists, and so forth. But in the end, my aim is to offer *Christian* resources for understanding and battling apathy.

The first chapter explores how pervasive apathy is in society, our churches, and our own hearts. Without providing a more detailed definition quite yet, I make some initial observations about the curious nature of apathy and gesture toward the hope of overcoming it. Chapter 2 attempts to define apathy by integrating wisdom from philosophers, theologians, psychologists, and more. This chapter requires us to slow down and think carefully about the concept of apathy, but hopefully the clarity achieved will be worth the effort. The third chapter addresses some possible causes of apathy. My aim is to help us diagnose the sources that seem most true to our experiences individually. There are certainly other causes, but these are a helpful starting point. Chapter 4 brings our apathy into conversation with the gospel. How does the good news of God's grace confront the apathetic? The chapter highlights the liberating truth that God is the main actor in the fight against apathy. It is he who offers hope and healing from chronic indifference. The final chapter turns our attention to what *we* can do to help foster anti-apathy postures in our lives. While God and his gospel are the primary players, we are by no means mere spectators. Discipline, intentionality, and work (gasp!) are essential for the cultivation of virtues that will help keep apathy at bay.

May this little book be an instrument in God's hands to nudge you one step further away from indifference.

1

A Show about Nothing

Our Culture of Apathy

IMAGINE YOU DIED and your children discovered your secret journals—what would they find within? What would surprise them? What themes would stick out to them? In my case, I think my kids would be overwhelmed by the number of entries in which I prayed the same kind of prayer: "Lord, wake me up!"

I became a Christian when I was eighteen, after wrestling with the fear of death for some time. I met Jesus through reading the Gospel of Matthew in a King James Bible given to me as a birthday gift. Reading of Jesus's character, seeing his love in action, and encountering for the first time his promises of eternal life were absolutely transformative. Without hearing a formal "gospel presentation," I was powerfully drawn to him. I decided in the course of my reading that I wanted to follow this man for the rest of my life. I finally found hope.

My early days as a Christian were marked by youthful zeal. I remember taking forty-five-minute walks home from high school, rather than hopping on the school bus, just so I could stop at the local Christian bookstore (remember those?) to browse books about the Bible. I'd chitchat with the store manager, asking question after question about good books to read. I had a hunger to know things I knew nothing about. When I got home from school, I'd scurry up to my room for time alone with God, the Bible, and whatever book I had picked up from the shop. Everything was different.

Or so I thought.

It didn't take long for me to feel in my gut that something wasn't right about my Christian life. I noticed a war raging inside of me. On the one hand, I had a strong desire for learning, truth, knowledge, understanding. On the other hand, I had started to feel "blah" about prayer, people, and other things that are supposed to matter to Christians.

This two-sidedness, or (better) double-mindedness, plagued me into my twenties. In college, I got involved with a campus ministry that was committed to helping Christians grow and to teaching them how to share their faith with others. While being a part of this group was fantastic in many ways, it also exacerbated my troubles. There's nothing worse than being around a bunch of passionate and sincere people when you don't feel very passionate about things you know you should care deeply about.

Much to my shame, several times when I was sharing the gospel with fellow students, I found myself wanting the experience to be over. Keep in mind, most spiritual conversations I had on campus were friendly. It was rare to have a stressful, antagonistic gospel encounter. Yet, I wanted them to end—not all the time, but enough times to give me pause.

In my mid- to late twenties, I sat in church services countless times daydreaming or waiting for the preaching to end. It had nothing to do with the quality of the preaching—I've been around a lot of good preaching. Instead, there was something askew in my affections. I lacked passion.

In time, I would come to hate the word *passion*! But I couldn't fault those who had it. I was convinced they were on to something. Jesus's rebuke to the churches in Ephesus encapsulated how I felt about my Christian life, even in those early days: "I have this against you, that you have abandoned the love you had at first" (Rev. 2:4).

I was lame and lukewarm. So on top of filling journals with prayers of longing, I took up writing songs of desperation. A few verses from one song sheepishly exclaimed the theme that pervaded my journals:

Wake me up, I don't know that I'm sleeping,
Wake me up 'cause I'm dead unawares;
Wake me up 'cause I've fallen asleep,
And I don't care.

Wake me up 'cause my life seems a duty,
Wake me up 'cause I can't mean a prayer;
Wake me up 'cause I can't see Your beauty,
And I don't care.

This song summed up my twenties: apathy mixed with longing and a tinge of guilt.

Making Indifference Fashionable

Roughly coinciding with my becoming a Christian was the advent of *Seinfeld*. No TV show before or since has captivated me as much as this quirky sitcom from the 1990s. My Thursday nights were built around catching the latest episodes. I had never seen a show so clever, creative, and consistently hilarious. I wasn't alone in my love for the sitcom. During its last five seasons, 30 million or more viewers tuned in weekly, with the finale garnering around 76 million viewers. It is regularly cited as one of the best shows of all time and has remained a cultural phenomenon since going into syndication.

The brilliance of the show's concept was portrayed in a key episode in season four, where Jerry (played by Jerry Seinfeld) and George (played by Jason Alexander) discuss writing a TV show pilot episode for NBC. As they consider what the show might be about and exchange some typically witty banter, George timidly suggests, "This should be the show. This is the show."

Jerry: What?

George: This. Just talking.

Jerry: Yeah, right.

George: I'm really serious. I think that's a good idea.

Jerry: Just talking? What's the show about?

George: It's about nothing.

Jerry: No story?

George: No, forget the story.

Jerry: You gotta have a story!

George: Who says you gotta have a story?

As the conversation goes on and Jerry remains bewildered by the concept, he exclaims in a frustrated voice, "I still don't know what the idea is!"

George: It's about nothing!
Jerry: Right.
George: Everybody's doing something. We'll do nothing.
Jerry: So, we go into NBC, we tell them we got an idea for a show about nothing?
George: Exactly.
Jerry: They say, "What's your show about?" I say, "Nothing."
George: There you go!
[Pause . . .]
Jerry: I think you may have something here.[1]

This scene was a bit of an inside joke. The show's writers were giving the audience a behind-the-scenes glimpse into how Seinfeld and the sitcom's cocreator, Larry David, came up with and pitched the show. Though this may not have been the writers' intention, this scene suggested that a key to understanding the actual show (not the imaginary pilot) was to recognize that it was a "show about nothing."

Many fans latched on to the idea that *Seinfeld* was a show about nothing. The writers *were* onto something. A show about nothing was quite unique—uncharted waters even. But was *Seinfeld* really a show about *nothing*?

1   *Seinfeld*, season 4, episode 9, "The Pitch," directed by Tom Cherones, written by Larry David and Jerry Seinfeld, featuring Jerry Seinfeld, Julia Louis-Dreyfus, Jason Alexander, and Michael Richards, aired September 16, 1992.

The show's unofficial motto, "No hugging, no learning," coined by David, highlighted its nose-thumbing attitude toward previous TV and societal conventions. It was not a show about nothing *per se*, but a show about insignificant, petty things. It was a show that normalized indifference toward big, meaningful things (such as marriage, family, religion, social concern, even the Holocaust) and a fixation on life's daily minutia (such as getting a good parking spot, the annoyance of "close talkers," and maintaining one's high score in Frogger).

Indifference was the name of the game.

Nothing captured this theme like the series finale. While waiting around in the small fictional town of Latham, Massachusetts, the show's four main characters witness an overweight man getting carjacked. Rather than jumping to his aid, they sit back and mock him about his weight, video record the assault taking place, and then walk away. The victim notices their mockery and inaction, and eventually reports them to the officer on the scene. The four are then arrested for violating what is known as the "Good Samaritan Law," a statute requiring bystanders to respond in situations when others are in danger.

A lengthy and highly publicized trial ensues. The prosecutors call in witness after witness (characters from several previous episodes) to demonstrate that the main characters' inaction toward the carjacking victim is just one example among many of their poor character.

Finally, the judge calls on the jury to read its verdict on the charge of "criminal indifference." The jurors find Jerry and his friends guilty. But it is the judge's closing statement that captures the truth about *Seinfeld* that its writers and viewers have known (or at least felt) all along. He declares, "I don't know how or under what circumstances the four of you found each other, but your callous indifference and utter disregard for everything that is good and decent has rocked the very foundation upon which our society is built."

They are sentenced to one year in jail. The series ends with the four friends sitting in a jail cell, more or less indifferent to their consequences, chitchatting about the location of George's shirt button—which, not coincidentally, is the very thing he and Jerry talked about in the opening scene of the very first episode—among other insignificant things.

Thus concluded one of the best shows of all time, a show that ended as it began, with none of the characters really having grown as a person. *Seinfeld* made it fashionable to not care about significant things, to treat them with a "meh." As David would tell an interviewer, "A lot of people don't understand that *Seinfeld* is a dark show."[2]

A Seinfeldian Society

I wonder what effect being reared on *Seinfeld*, not to mention other shows, such as *The Simpsons*, *Married with Children*, and *Friends*, had on my posture toward life. While there were certainly a number of factors shaping me at the time, a steady diet of this kind of pop culture (and I watched *a lot* of TV) only nurtured an attitude of indifference. Subconsciously I grew to believe that it was cooler to not care about meaningful things, or at least to not put any earnestness on display.

I knew, in my head, that there were important things in the world to care about. However, I couldn't bring myself to care deeply enough about them or move toward them.

I don't believe I'm alone in this. I think that many of us experience this disconnect between head, heart, and hands. We know what

2   Francis Davis, "Recognition Humor," *The Atlantic Online* (December 1992), https://www.theatlantic.com/.

is good, right, and life-giving, but cannot seem to lift a finger to do anything about it. We know that a bit of quiet reflection would do us some good, but we hit "Play" on that fourth consecutive episode of whatever show we're into. We're aware that spending some time in worship with other believers might inspire us, but we'd rather sleep in (especially after our previous night's Netflix marathon). I am calling this the "curse of apathy," and many of us have been stricken by it. Conversations with friends, youth workers, my students, and colleagues have convinced me that we live in a culture plagued by apathy. For too many of us, life feels like a show about nothing. It feels unworthy of our serious attention. We are citizens of a Seinfeldian society, where only inconsequential things matter.

This claim may seem counterintuitive in light of how easily people seem to get outraged these days. Yet, I'm simply trying to shed light on the fact that we are numb to the meaningful, but often "alive" to the trivial.

Exhibit A: In 2010, the clothing retailer Gap decided to re-brand itself, changing its iconic blue box logo to something more "modern, sexy, cool." Company executives could not have foreseen the strong blowback the new logo received. Critics panned it, the Twittersphere mocked it, and Gap's Facebook page overflowed with comments deriding the redesign:

"THE NEW LOGO IS DISGUSTING!!"

"THE NEW LOGO IS HORRIBLE!!"

"NO NEW LOGO!! the old one is a BRAND . . . not just a NAME!!!"

"Sad, sad day for GAP!!! Old logo is classic and should stay put!!!"

"A monstrosity"

"I'll be surprised if a few people won't lose their jobs"

And on and on it went. There were hundreds of comments—some lighthearted, many disturbingly serious. It is amazing how passionate people can get about a company's logo! Gap learned this the hard way. After only six days and oodles of dollars spent, the company reverted to its previous logo design. Similar responses would follow Yahoo's redesign in 2013 (which it redesigned again in 2019).

Some things evoke passion in us, while other things induce yawns. The paradox of apathy is that we are captivated by the things we don't really care about and are lukewarm to the things that, in our heart of hearts, mean the most to us. We don't act on what we should act on, but we are awakened to things we should probably ignore.

Thus, busyness and activity are not necessarily the antonyms to apathy. What one writer says about sloth is true of apathy: "It easily attaches to our hectic and overburdened schedules. We appear to be anything but slothful (read: apathetic), yet that is exactly what we are, as we do more and care less, and feel pressured to do still more."[3]

While I have chosen not to define apathy until the next chapter, I've sought here to focus on its strange selectivity. It is not

---

3 Kathleen Norris, *Acedia & Me: A Marriage, Monks, and a Writer's Life* (New York: Riverhead, 2008), 130.

care-less; it is care-adrift, care-misplaced. As another writer puts it, our culture is a "breeding ground" for chronic apathy due to the proliferation of distractions available to us.[4] We are regularly invited to care, just not too much or about too important a matter. In fact, our busyness may serve only to exacerbate our disengagement from meaning and to keep our spirits in a state of lethargy.[5]

It is not that our culture is unique in this. I imagine apathy has existed since the dawn of time. What seems unique is that apathy has to some degree become normalized and acceptable, and confessing it can be a mark of authenticity. There's no shame, no stigma attached to it in some quarters. At worst it's a bummer, but it is just the furniture of life in the twenty-first century.

Apathy and the Church

This issue is all the more important for Christians, who know the only true God, have Jesus as their Savior, have been given a mission to the world, and are promised eternal life. In other words, we've been given access to the most significant realities one could imagine. Yet, we "are in the world" even if we're not of it. The things that pervade our society inevitably creep into the church and shape the people of God. Apathy is no different.

Sometimes it seems as if there's some sort of inverse relationship between the grandeur of a truth and our emotional and practical response to it. The greater the truth (or concept or calling), the less we care about it. Perhaps this is a result of the fact that sermons and Bible studies never stop talking about

---

4 Nicole M. Roccas, *Time and Despondency: Regaining the Present in Faith and Life* (Chesterton, IN: Ancient Faith, 2017), 18.

5 Norris, *Acedia & Me*, 131.

the biggest things, like God and salvation, heaven and hell. Maybe grand things have become too common, too familiar. Yet, whatever the reason may be, we are bored by big things; the bigger, the more boring.

Over sixty-five years ago, A. W. Tozer bemoaned the evangelical devotion to what he called "the great god Entertainment." In a provocative essay, he observes how the broader culture's fixation on amusement and entertainment has corrupted the church. He writes, "For centuries the Church stood solidly against every form of worldly entertainment, recognizing it for what it was—a device for wasting time, a refuge from the disturbing voice of conscience, a scheme to divert attention from moral accountability." He goes on to say that rather than continuing the battle against the great god Entertainment and suffering the abuse that attends the struggle, the church has joined forces with him. Then he gets especially prickly (and this is worth quoting at length):

> So today we have the astonishing spectacle of millions of dollars being poured into the unholy job of providing earthly entertainment for the so-called sons of heaven. Religious entertainment is in many places rapidly crowding out the serious things of God. Many churches these days have become little more than poor theatres where fifth-rate "producers" peddle their shoddy wares with the full approval of evangelical leaders who can even quote a holy text in defense of their delinquency. And hardly a man dares raise his voice against it.[6]

6 A. W. Tozer, *The Root of the Righteous* (Harrisburg, PA: Christian Publications, 1955), 32–33.

To think that Tozer was saying this in the 1950s! If this was true then, what would he say about our times? We care about things that do not matter. We devote ourselves to amusement. We worship at the altar of the trivial, and Tozer's point is that we would be far from apathetic if someone were to speak against our devotion to this great god.

A recent article entitled "Local Christian Counting on Kingdom of God as Backup Plan Just in Case Favorite Political Party Fails Him" reads,

LAKE CHARLES, LA—Local Christian Guy Tenney announced Monday that he's still clinging to the hope of the coming of the Kingdom of God, just in case his political party happens to fail him.

"On the off chance that my political party doesn't usher in peace on earth, I guess there's always Jesus," he said thoughtfully as he opened his Bible for morning devotions, but spent most of the time checking the Twitter feeds of his favorite political pundits to see on which front the culture war would be fought today. "It's good to have a plan B to fall back on."

Tenney said, however, that he doesn't expect his chosen political party to fail him. He pointed out that they have money, power, and the promise to use the government to do stuff that he approves of.[7]

This is, of course, satire from the website *The Babylon Bee*, which makes a living pointing to ironies in Christians' priorities. Much of its humor revolves around our shared sense that

---

7 "Local Christian Counting on Kingdom of God as Backup Plan Just in Case Favorite Political Party Fails Him," *The Babylon Bee*, July 8, 2019, https://babylonbee.com/.

Christians often get exercised by things that don't matter, but are indifferent to things that should move them. Other delightfully funny headlines include:

"Baptist Church Service Halftime Show Criticized for Showing Too Much Ankle"

"Christian Not Sure Why He Should Look Forward to Heaven When He Already Lives in America"

"Christian Artist Renounces Faith Now That Jesus Has Served His Purpose of Providing Fame, Fortune"

It would be an unfair overstatement to claim that the church doesn't care at all about important things. Rather, I think the issue is often the two-sidedness I spoke of earlier: we care on some deep level, but don't care enough to be moved; we know what the good is, but often do not find it very exciting or engaging.

Here's a quiz: Which of these core Christian practices would you say your church is passionate about?

Scripture Engagement—Does your congregation read the Scriptures regularly, value the Word, apply it, obey it, and speak it? Is the Bible a central part of church life?

Prayer—Is your community characterized by prayer, not just during services but throughout the week? Does more than 5 percent of your church body show up to prayer meetings, if you have those at all?

Generosity—Is your community known for extravagant generosity rather than for being consumers? Are people organizing their lives around giving rather than the pursuit of more success and wealth? Is the generosity that is evident in your church so compelling that it draws others to Christ?

Church Involvement—Does the average church member attend church three or even (gasp) four times a month? Is *committed* a word you would use to characterize the people of your congregation?

Evangelism—Would you describe your church or immediate Christian community as thoughtfully engaged in introducing others to Jesus Christ?

Mission—Does the average person in your church know what the Great Commission is? If so, when was the last time your church talked about its strategy for contributing to the fulfillment of the Great Commission? Can you name some missionaries sent by your church? How often do the needs of the broader world take center stage?[8]

Again, our communities *do* care about a number of important things, and I don't want to diminish that. I'm confident our churches are doing well in some of these areas, average in a few,

8   Categories regarding Bible reading are borrowed from Kenneth Berding, *Bible Revival: Recommitting Ourselves to One Book* (Bellingham, WA: Lexham, 2013). Questions regarding giving are taken from the Generous Giving website: https://generousgiving.org/who-we-are.

and poorly in others. Yet most of us would likely not characterize our communities as zealous and earnest. The research bears this out.

We typically hover in the realm of the so-so. For example, among evangelicals (characteristically Bible-loving people), only 49 percent of people read "at least a bit" of the Bible daily. This number dips to 16 percent for nonevangelicals. Another survey shows that among Protestant churchgoers, 40 percent engage with Scripture once per week (on average) or less.[9]

Now I'm not a huge fan of using statistics to make Christians feel horrible about themselves and their communities. I include these numbers simply to highlight that the church—the pillar and foundation of the truth, according to the apostle Paul (1 Tim. 3:15 CSB)—is sometimes perplexingly sluggish about the very things that make it what it is.

Me and My Shadow

It is far too tempting to point fingers at the church and assume that its indifference is due to poor leadership, lame preaching, a lack of opportunities, the ethos, or whatever. These factors can contribute, but the apathy of the church is more likely just a mirror image of the apathy in each individual member's heart. It is not a "they" problem.

As a theology professor, when I stand before fifty students to teach them about the doctrine of justification, sanctification, or the resurrection, and I am more enthusiastic about finding out

9   Bob Smietana, "LifeWay Research: Americans Are Fond of the Bible, Don't Actually Read It," LifeWay Research, April 25, 2017; Aaron Earls, "Few Protestant Churchgoers Read the Bible Daily," LifeWay Research, July 2, 2019, https://lifewayresearch.com/.

the score in Manchester United's afternoon match, it is not a "they" problem.

Likewise, when students or friends tell me, "I haven't read my Bible in weeks," "I'm struggling to pray," "I don't go to church very often," or "I played Fortnite for five hours last night with my roommates," I am certain that it is not a "they" problem. Apathy is an "I" problem, a sickness unto death in many of our own hearts.

For some of us, apathy feels like a shadow, a companion we just can't shake. It goes wherever we go and clouds our Christian lives. As much as it pervades the church, what we really need to attend to is that it is not first *their* shadow or even *our* shadow, but *my* shadow. I must attend to it as mine before I try to deal with it in others. Apathy is the log in *my* eye.

So far, I've attempted to provide a number of pictures of apathy, and I have had at least two purposes in doing this. First, I want us to see ourselves in the variety of images and illustrations I've drawn from our culture and the church. We are products of *and* contributors to the malaise in our various communities. The prophet Isaiah said, "I am a man of unclean lips, and I dwell in the midst of a people of unclean lips" (Isa. 6:5). In the same way, we must each confess, "I am a man (or woman) of indifference, and I dwell in the midst of a people of indifference." We need to be honest *with* ourselves *about* ourselves. Second, and more important, I want us to see that we are not alone in our apathy. Many people, particularly in the church, are trying to make sense of their indifference and, hopefully, overcome it. This process of identifying with others is a crucial, but preliminary, step to understanding and dealing with our apathy.

Yet we also need a clear vision of what exactly we are called to and hope that we can actually fulfill that calling. What is God's expectation of us? Is it reasonable and realistic? Can we meet his demands?

Knowledge without Zeal

When we think of the opposite of apathy, we might immediately think of the word *passion*. One author describes passion as the reality of being affected by something and as the "essential energy of the soul."[10] The apathetic know the feeling of lacking in energy, of feeling sleepy. But while *passion* is a perfectly fine word (especially since apathy could be defined literally as "without passion"), it is sometimes overused to the point of sounding like Christianese. My preferred term would be *zeal*, a biblical word that perhaps has less American cultural baggage and few of the negative connotations associated with passion throughout the Bible.

Zeal, like passion, is about being awakened again to the meaningful. If you've ever read the children's story *The Secret Garden*, you'll recall how the morose and numb protagonist, Mary Lennox, is enchanted out of her slumber by her encounter with the garden. She moves from unfeeling to being nearly obsessed with the garden to becoming a softened, engaged, alive little girl. That is the power of being affected by something. It energizes the soul. One also recalls Anne Shirley of Green Gables fame, one of my family's favorite literary characters, who is entirely incapable of being unaffected by the wonder and the woes of the world. In

10 Brennan Manning, *Abba's Child: The Cry of the Heart for Intimate Belonging* (Colorado Springs: NavPress, 1994), 117.

her own peculiar way, she is the antiapathy exemplar, one who is often perplexed by people who are not as moved by life as she is.

The apostle Paul describes Israel as those who "have a zeal for God, but not according to knowledge" (Rom. 10:2). Their zeal was misdirected, unenlightened, lacking a proper knowledge of God and his ways. The inverse is true of us. We are those who "have a knowledge of God, but not according to zeal." We often have a clear understanding of God, but lack a zeal consistent with that knowledge. Ignorance is not our issue. The heart is the heart of the matter.

One of the classic biblical examples of zeal is found in the story of Phinehas, the grandson of Aaron, in Numbers 25. The story takes place during Israel's wanderings in the wilderness. Israelite men begin to indulge in sexual immorality with Moabite women and give themselves over to the gods of Moab. This provokes the Lord's anger against his people. He sends a plague upon them, then commands Moses to kill the Israelite leaders (presumably those involved in the immorality) as an act of atonement for their evil. While the people are weeping over their sin and the Lord's judgment, a brash Israelite man brings a Midianite woman into the camp in plain view of all the people, totally disregarding the seriousness of the situation. This is where Phinehas comes in. He follows the couple into the man's tent and drives a spear into both the man and the woman. This bold act serves to lift the plague after it has killed twenty-four thousand people. Listen to how the Lord commends Phinehas's actions:

Phinehas son of Eleazar, the son of Aaron, the priest, has turned my anger away from the Israelites. Since he was as zealous for my honor among them as I am, I did not put an end to them in my zeal. Therefore tell him I am making my covenant of peace with him. He and his descendants will have a covenant of a lasting priesthood, because he was zealous for the honor of his God and made atonement for the Israelites. (Num. 25:11–13 NIV)

At least four things are worth noting about zeal from the Lord's words here. It (1) is a feeling deep inside someone that (2) leads to action; (3) is enacted on behalf of something or someone else that is deemed valuable (i.e., it is done out of love); and (4) reflects God's own character. While other Israelites were saddened by the consequences being visited upon their community, only Phinehas was roused to action. Rather than putting his hands in his pockets and merely hoping for the best, he aligned his actions with his values. He imitated the God who always moves on the things that matter most.

This way of characterizing zeal is consistent throughout Scripture. In a psalm that is used to describe Jesus's action of clearing the temple (John 2:17), the psalmist writes, "For zeal for your house has consumed me, / and the reproaches of those who reproach you have fallen on me" (Ps. 69:9). Elsewhere we read, "My zeal consumes me, / because my foes forget your words" (119:139). The prophet Elijah laments, "I have been very zealous for the LORD God Almighty. The Israelites have rejected your covenant, torn down your altars, and put your prophets to death with the sword" (1 Kings 19:10 NIV). Paul exhorts those who lead to do so with zeal (Rom. 12:8) and shortly thereafter instructs the whole church, "Do not be slothful in zeal, be fervent in spirit, serve the

Lord" (v. 11). Zeal is spiritual intensity; it is the opposite of apathy and sloth (a topic we'll discuss in the next chapter).

Now, these examples and exhortations from Scripture are good news for the apathetic, for they imply that zeal is possible; it is not merely for the few, the chosen.

The Greatest Generation(s)

We need examples and models, people who have resisted the devil of indifference and come out the other side. My wife and I often wonder if there is a real difference between our generation and those gone by. I have a fascination with what is known as the Greatest Generation—those born between 1901 and 1927, who survived the great wars and the Great Depression. This generation consisted of famous people like George H. W. Bush and Julia Child, as well as the millions of others who served as laborers, soldiers, and grunt workers during the Second World War. One writer sums up their achievements this way:

> In addition to enduring this country's greatest economic catastrophe and fighting two wars, they went on to work at Leviton and Boeing, they built homes and raised families in Omaha and Bakersfield. They put a man on the moon! They were carpenters, teachers, welders, Fuller Brush men. But, most important, they wove the fabric that made the United States great. They gave their children safe and secure homes; they exemplified a solid work ethic and belief in America; they instilled in their children the value of education.[11]

11 Richard Sousa, "The Greatest Generation," Hoover Institution, November 9, 2010, https://www.hoover.org/.

It was the toughness, fortitude, strength of character, conviction, and work ethic that made this group so remarkable. They were alive to the evils of the world, alive to their responsibility, and alive to the call for action. It is not that they were the only generation to display any of these attributes, but that these characteristics were forged in the toughest of circumstances and coalesced in this particular generation at such an important time in America's history.

I also wonder if there is a Greatest Generation of Christians, people whose grit, conviction, and effort make them worthy of emulation, especially in an age of distraction and indifference. My mind is immediately drawn to a figure such as Jonathan Edwards, the eighteenth-century preacher and theologian, who as a young man wrote seventy resolutions to help keep his spiritual life focused, energetic, and God-centered. He challenged himself to read them every week. Resolution #3 reads, "Resolved, if ever I shall fall and grow dull, so as to neglect to keep any part of these Resolutions, to repent of all I can remember, when I come to myself again." His sixth resolution: "Resolved, to live with all my might, while I do live."[12] Edwards is my go-to example of nonpassivity in the fight against dullness and indifference. As someone who regularly taught the truth of God—in fact, as one of the greatest minds in American history—he recognized that the heart is always the issue. He knew that those exposed to the richest Christian truths often find themselves cold to those very truths. Remember, apathy is often dull to the most meaningful things; the greater the truths, the more we yawn.

---

12 Jonathan Edwards, "Resolutions," in *The Works of Jonathan Edwards*, vol. 16, *Letters and Personal Writings*, ed. George S. Claghorn (New Haven: Yale University Press, 1998), 753–59.

But are there exemplars closer to our day that call us higher and give us hope that zeal is possible? Certainly! I'm sure there are at least a handful of saints we each could list as models of conviction and Christian zeal. Think of Brother Andrew, the Dutch missionary who smuggled Bibles behind the Iron Curtain for decades. Or Jim Elliot and his friends, who were arrested by the call to take the gospel to one of the darkest corners of the earth—a call that led to their deaths.

Yet zeal is not necessarily about becoming a missionary or martyr (at least not literally). Zeal in the day-to-day is about being alive to the important things around us. It is about being awake to God, aware of his presence and calling especially in those hidden moments of our day. Thus, zeal can take many seemingly mundane shapes, such as:

- going to bed on time, so that we don't just lapse into our morning;
- committing to being with God's people every Sunday;
- being inclined to say yes when asked to provide meals for church members, be on the clean-up crew after a large event, or give someone a ride to the airport;
- working hard, when one form of engaging Scripture begins to grow stale, to find other ways to feed on the word (e.g., sermons, audio Bibles, Scripture memory songs, etc.);
- dedicating ourselves to praying regularly for specific missionaries; or
- devoting ourselves to understanding cultural issues with care and nuance.

Notice that most, if not all, of these things are done in secret and don't necessarily favor the extrovert. Introverts are welcome.

Zeal is commitment to love and pursue the good, even when it hurts or when no one else sees. And that possibility is open to us all.

Rather than making us feel small and lame, the examples of Edwards, Andrew, and Elliot, as well as ordinary believers, point us to the possibility that we can change. Countless brothers and sisters in Christ wake up most days with energy and commitment to not sleepwalk through their spiritual lives. Their zeal can become our zeal. You may not feel that way because your "shadow," apathy, has followed you for so long. Nevertheless, it is true—you *can* change. You can move from indifference to fervor, from pajamas to purpose.

A Prayer of Hope

So, pause and ask yourself: Where does apathy show up most in my life? What areas does it plague? How does apathy hinder me from living a full, kingdom of God kind of life? What I've been seeking to do in this chapter is to help us see, own, and confess our sickness so as to put ourselves on the path of healing (see James 5:16). The Lord restores the contrite and brokenhearted (Pss. 34:18; 147:3; Isa. 66:2). God can wake us up from a life that feels like a show about nothing.

I'd like to close with a prayer I come back to over and over again in various seasons of my spiritual life. This title prayer from the book of Puritan prayers called *The Valley of Vision* is all about the paradoxes of the Christian life.[13] To some degree, this chapter has also been about paradox, the paradox of apathy—that we engage with vigor the things

---

13 William Bennett, *The Valley of Vision: A Collection of Puritan Prayers and Devotions* (Carlisle, PA: Banner of Truth, 2002), xxiv–xxv. Used with permission.

that are peripheral and are bored by the things that are at the core of who we are. But this prayer is about the only paradox that matters in our fight against apathy—the paradox of grace.

Lord, High and Holy, Meek and Lowly,

Thou hast brought me to the valley of vision,
where I live in the depths but see thee in the heights;
hemmed in by mountains of sin I behold thy glory.

Let me learn by paradox
that the way down is the way up,
that to be low is to be high,
that the broken heart is the healed heart,
that the contrite spirit is the rejoicing spirit,
that the repenting soul is the victorious soul,
that to have nothing is to possess all,
that to bear the cross is to wear the crown,
that to give is to receive,
that the valley is the place of vision.

Lord, in the daytime stars can be seen from deepest wells,
and the deeper the wells the brighter thy stars shine;
Let me find thy light in my darkness,
thy life in my death,
thy joy in my sorrow,
thy grace in my sin,
thy riches in my poverty,
thy glory in my valley.

I hope you find encouragement and hope, knowing that God is with us, even in the valley of apathy.

Questions for Reflection

1. Do you tend to focus on apathy in (1) the culture, (2) the church, or (3) your own life?

2. What about apathy (the culture's, church's, or your own) do you find most troubling?

3. Before reading further, it might be helpful to conjure up a picture in your mind of what you think passion/zeal looks like. What might it look like for you in your daily life?

2

The Noonday Demon

On the Concept of Apathy

KIM PHILBY WAS A BRITISH SPY during the Second World War and the early years of the Cold War. He was a charming figure who quickly rose to the highest ranks of the British intelligence community as a major leader within MI6. Philby came from the right circles—educated at the elite Westminster School and then Cambridge—and was able to make friends in all the right places, including high-ranking members of both the British and American intelligence establishments.

In the late 1940s, suspicions arose surrounding certain British intelligence workers. It would be discovered that five men—known as the Cambridge Five—were really Soviet operatives masquerading as British intelligence agents and passing on British and American military secrets to the USSR. Philby was among the five. He had been recruited by the Soviets shortly after graduating from Cambridge and had remained undetected for more than fifteen years (and not discovered with certainty until the early 1960s). Ben Macintrye's book *A Spy among Friends* captures how Philby deceptively developed close friendships with a fellow MI6 officer and a CIA agent. Unbeknownst to them, he was passing along accounts of every conversation with them to Moscow.

Philby is now famous as one of history's greatest spies—celebrated in Moscow after his defection and despised in the Western intelligence community for undermining its work for nearly two decades. No one would have thought this charming British citizen was working to destroy the Western way of life.[1]

There is a famous saying, "Know the enemy and know yourself; in a hundred battles you will never be in peril."[2] Knowledge is power in the context of a battle. The extreme lengths to which Philby and the Cambridge Five were willing to go to destroy the West underscores the value of knowing one's enemy. The clearer we are about our foe, the more likely we will be to defeat him.

Apathy is an enemy of the soul. Since this book seeks to help those struggling with apathy, it's important to define our terms—in other words, to know our adversary. My working assumption so far has been that those who experience apathy or see others with apathy know what it is even if they can't define it. However, I want to move us toward a clearer notion of what apathy is so we will be able to battle it more effectively. We'll work our way toward a definition by having several important conversations—with ancient philosophers, ancient monks and theologians, psychologists and

---

1 Ben Macintrye, *A Spy among Friends: Kim Philby and the Great Betrayal* (New York: Crown, 2014).

2 Sun Tzu, *The Art of War*, trans. Samuel B. Griffiths (Oxford: Oxford University Press, 1971), 84.

psychiatrists, and apathy's "cousins" (depression, despondency, and dry spells). Some of this discussion may be challenging. Defining things often demands extra care and mental energy. But the payoff will be greater clarity on what exactly we're dealing with. My hope is that, as conversations were ammunition for Philby and his associates, the insights gained from these conversations will become weapons in our fight against apathy.

Virtuous Indifference

Our first conversation is with ancient philosophers. The concept of apathy has a long history in the Western world. We are not the only culture to treat it as "cool." The great philosophers of the past debated its meaning and value. In fact, among certain Greek philosophers, apathy was one of the greatest things one could aspire to. The Greek term *apatheia* means "without *pathē*" (passions), and in the thought of some philosophers, passions often referred to violent emotions such as love, fear, grief, anger, envy, lust, pain, or pleasure that arise as responses to the outside world. According to the Stoics, for instance, the wise—those who desire a life of flourishing—are totally free from passions. In other words, the wise are not vulnerable to the ups and downs of life in this world. They are self-sufficient; the external happenings of life "merely graze the surface" of their minds.[3] The goal of life is what we might call "equanimity" or a calmness of soul.

The point of this first conversation is simply to highlight that apathy was at one time a supremely valued orientation toward life. Even great non-Stoic philosophers such as Aristotle acknowledged

3   Martha Nussbaum, *The Therapy of Desire: Theory and Practice in Hellenistic Ethics* (Princeton: Princeton University Press, 1994), 390.

the value of limiting the passions, for the good life was thought to await the apathetic.

Apathetic God, Apathetic People

Now let's chat with ancient monks and theologians. Early Christian thinkers were well aware of the ancient philosophical tradition of thought that valued apathy. Interestingly, like their philosophical forebears, they sought to apply the concept of *apatheia* not only to human beings, but also to God.

Is there something we can call divine apathy? Those who have taken an introductory course in theology might have encountered the term *impassibility* in discussions about God's attributes. "Impassibility" is simply a Latin translation of the Greek term *apatheia*, and it was a concept much discussed among the church fathers. According to one scholar, to speak of God as impassible is to say that "he does not have the same emotions as the gods of the heathen; that his care for human beings is free from self-interest and any association with evil." Impassibility means that God is not overwhelmed by emotions, and neither are his emotions affected by anything outside himself.[4] While it may be appropriate to ascribe "emotions" to God, impassibility (or divine *apatheia*) rules out those that are unbecoming of him. So, for example, when we speak of God as love, we really are speaking of a passionate God. But it is an impassible passion, a love not dictated by the outside world. In other words, God is not subject to violent passions as we are. *Apatheia* is another way of speaking of the unchangeableness and steadfastness of God's affection for all that he is and all that he has made.

4   Paul Gavrilyuk, *The Suffering of the Impassible God: The Dialectics of Patristic Thought*, Oxford Early Christian Studies (Oxford: Oxford University Press, 2004), 15–16.

How does this understanding of divine *apatheia* relate to human apathy? According to some thinkers in the ancient church, human apathy is a virtuous state of being and an imaging of God's own virtue. A person who has *apatheia* has ruled his or her passions through discipline and attained a true love of God.[5] According to Evagrius of Pontus, a fourth-century monk, "Love is the offspring of impassibility."[6] He goes on to say several flattering things about apathy:

The kingdom of heaven is *apathy* of the soul . . .

Apathy is the health of the soul . . .

Perfect *apathy* emerges in the soul after the victory over all the demons that oppose the practical [disciplined] life.

When [the soul] has acquired *apathy*, it will easily recognize the artifices [schemes] of the enemies.[7]

This conversation highlights that early church thinkers, like some philosophers of the past, viewed *apatheia* as virtuous—either as freedom from passions or as constancy in love for God and others. It was something to be sought, the culmination of an examined, chastened, and well-ordered life.

5 Gavrilyuk, *Suffering of the Impassible God*, 15.

6 *Evagrius of Pontus: The Greek Ascetic Corpus*, trans. Robert E. Sinkewicz, Oxford Early Christian Studies (Oxford: Oxford University Press, 2003), 110.

7 *Evagrius of Pontus*, 96–111 (emphasis added). I've exchanged the translation "impassibility" with "apathy" to help make the point.

Apathy as Vice

Let us continue our conversation with ancient monks and theologians as we consider a more negative understanding of apathy. *Apatheia* doesn't appear to be the way forward in understanding apathy as we know it. The kind of apathy we deal with is not about consciously trying to steel ourselves against the ups and downs of life or about trying to cultivate a detachment from the world that produces a love for God. We need to look elsewhere for help. I believe the early Christian concept that best overlaps with what we would call apathy is not *apatheia*, but a less-than-savory term—*sloth* (or *acedia*). When we think of sloth, we may think of a slow-moving creature, or a couch potato who spends all day in pajamas eating pints of Ben and Jerry's. However, Christians described sloth in a far richer way, and we might find it useful in trying to get our minds around what apathy is all about.

Acedia is a Greek term that literally means "indifference, lethargy, exhaustion, and apathy." One of the earliest and most influential thinkers on acedia was Evagrius of Pontus, whom we've already encountered. He compiled a list of eight deadly temptations that later morphed into what we know as the seven deadly sins. Although he is unknown to many of us, and we don't often find ourselves conversing with monks, his reflections are insightful into the spiritual dimensions of apathy. Let's begin with a rich but lengthy definition:

Acedia is an ethereal friendship, one who leads our steps astray, hatred of industriousness, a battle against stillness, stormy weather for psalmody, laziness in prayer, a slackening of ascesis [strict self-discipline], untimely drowsiness, revolving sleep, the oppressiveness of solitude, hatred of one's cell, an adversary of ascetic works, an opponent of perseverance, a muzzling of meditation, ignorance of the scriptures, a partaker in sorrow.[8]

Does any of this sound familiar? Even though he is writing to fellow monks—whose days (unlike ours) consisted of spending long hours in solitary cells, praying, meditating on the Psalms, and doing various forms of manual labor—I think we can relate to what he's describing here.[9] Acedia is a constant companion. It targets the spiritual practices that are supposed to bring us life, such as prayer, stillness, Scripture reading, hard work, and perseverance in doing good. In his practical instructions to fellow monks about various vices, he devotes more space to describing acedia than any other. He describes it as "the noonday demon" (drawing on Ps. 91:6), the worst of all the demons (i.e., the vices), typically attacking its victim between 10 a.m. and 2 p.m. It compels a person to resist hard work, despise his station in life, and believe the lie that no one cares enough to console him in sorrow.[10] Acedia is a "relaxation of soul," something like a laziness of mind. A person with acedia lacks diligence; he performs spiritual things just to get them over and done with.

---

8 *Evagrius of Pontus*, 64.
9 See Greg Peters, *The Monkhood of All Believers: The Monastic Foundation of Christian Spirituality* (Grand Rapids, MI: Baker Academic, 2018), 2–9.
10 *Evagrius of Pontus*, 99.

Here's what Evagrius says about how those with acedia approach reading (if this doesn't sound like our devotional times, I don't know what does!):

> When he reads, the one afflicted with acedia yawns a lot and readily drifts off into sleep; he rubs his eyes and stretches his arms; turning his eyes away from the book, he stares at the wall and again goes back to reading for awhile; leafing through the pages, he looks curiously for the end of texts. . . . Later, he closes the book and puts it under his head and falls asleep.[11]

Again, what is striking is that he is writing to those who have devoted their lives to study and serving the Lord. These men, for whatever reason (likely because they are hungry, lonely, and in need of sunshine), seem especially prone to acedia. The noonday demon fosters a boredom concerning the very things that define the monastic life.

Similarly, another monk and important thinker, John Cassian, describes acedia as a restlessness that entices us to pursue everything but our most important duties. Acedia distracts. It makes us lazy and sluggish toward our spiritual and practical responsibilities. It is a selective laziness that makes everything *else* appealing.[12]

So, is acedia (or sloth) a sin? The great theologian Thomas Aquinas answers this question with a resounding yes. He describes

11 *Evagrius of Pontus*, 84.
12 John Cassian, *Institutes of the Coenobia* X.II, in *Nicene and Post-Nicene Fathers of the Christian Church*, Second Series, ed. Philip Schaff and Henry Wace (New York: Christian Literature Co., 1894), 11:267.

sloth as "an oppressive sorrow" that "so weighs upon a man's mind, that he wants to do nothing." This sorrow is always evil when it is about something that is good in reality. Sloth is a lack of joy in and love for what's truly good.[13] Ultimately, sloth is apathy toward God, the things of God, and the life of God in us. As one writer summarizing Thomas's view puts it, "The slothful person . . . is one who resists the effort of doing day after day whatever it takes to keep the bonds of love strong and living and healthy, whether he or she feels particularly inspired about doing it or not."[14] Sloth is a spiritual sickness; it is the old self doing battle with the new self and resisting its advances.[15] Thus, it is a sin.

If acedia remains unacknowledged and undealt with, it will only fester and foster greater disinterest. C. S. Lewis insightfully captures this dimension of acedia in one of the correspondences in *The Screwtape Letters*. He describes the slothful as hovering between ignorance of their sin and full repentance. They have a vague and uneasy feeling that they're not doing well, but they do nothing about it—and this is precisely where Satan wants to keep them. This unaddressed dis-ease is perfect soil for the devil to do his work. Screwtape (the experienced demon) thus counsels Wormwood (the inexperienced demon),

> If such a feeling is allowed to live, but not allowed to become
> irresistible and flower into real repentance, it has one invaluable

---

13 Thomas Aquinas, *Summa Theologica*, 2nd. rev. ed., trans. Fathers of the English Dominican Province (1920; New Advent, 2008), 2.35.1, https://www.newadvent .org/.

14 Rebecca Konyndyk DeYoung, *Glittering Vices: A New Look at the Seven Deadly Sins and Their Remedies* (Grand Rapids, MI: Brazos, 2009), 86–87.

15 DeYoung, *Glittering Vices*, 89.

tendency. It increases the patient's reluctance to think about the Enemy [i.e., God]. All humans at nearly all times have some such reluctance; but when thinking of Him involves facing and intensifying a whole vague cloud of half-conscious guilt, this reluctance is increased tenfold. . . . In this state your patient will not omit, but he will increasingly dislike, his religious duties. He will think about them as little as he feels he decently can beforehand, and forget them as soon as possible when they are over. A few weeks ago you had to *tempt* him to unreality and inattention in his prayers: but now you will find him opening his arms to you and almost begging you to distract his purpose and benumb his heart. He will *want* his prayers to be unreal, for he will dread nothing so much as effective contact with the Enemy. His aim will be to let sleeping worms lie.[16]

Is this not what Thomas, Cassian, and Evagrius were describing? The slothful are reluctant to face their religious duties; they do the bare minimum; they harbor a relative dislike for God; they ignore prayer; they long for distraction. Like me in my early twenties, they walk around in a fog of guilt. What Lewis captures so well is that acedia is a weapon of our enemy and that the struggle against sloth is a spiritual battle.

One recent writer helpfully sums up acedia, pointing out that it can take different forms in different people. For example, it can manifest as (1) restlessness, the inability to complete a book, pray at length, or finish a task; (2) productivity accompanied by anger or boredom over the things one is doing; or (3) an inclination to

16 C. S. Lewis, *The Screwtape Letters* (New York: HarperCollins, 2001), 58–59.

sleeping, eating, worrying, and distraction.[17] A common thread weaving these various manifestations together is purposelessness or aimlessness. Things are either left undone, done for the wrong purpose, or done for no purpose whatsoever. The heart is numb to the "demands of love,"[18] that is, the things God has called us to. Dorothy Sayers calls acedia "the sin which believes in nothing, cares for nothing, seeks to know nothing, interferes with nothing, enjoys nothing, loves nothing, hates nothing, finds purpose in nothing, lives for nothing, and only remains alive because there is nothing it would die for."[19] This is purposeless, aimless indifference.

As we wrap up this particular conversation, I hope we can see that acedia, as Christians have thought about it through the ages, is really a helpful category for understanding what we know as apathy. As a diagnosis of the soul, it points to the fact that whatever is going on in us is not merely psychological or emotional, but also spiritual. In fact, acedia seems to be characterized most by its resistance to the spiritual. And isn't that what we find so troubling about apathy?

A Real Psychological Syndrome?

But so much for acedia—for now. As we try to get our minds around our various spiritual pathologies—such as apathy—contemporary psychology and psychiatry may also prove

---

17   Nicole M. Roccas, *Time and Despondency: Regaining the Present in Faith and Life* (Chesterton, IN: Ancient Faith, 2017).

18   DeYoung, *Glittering Vices*, 79.

19   Dorothy L. Sayers, *Creed or Chaos? Why Christians Must Choose Either Dogma or Disaster* (Manchester: Sophia Institute, 1999), 148.

helpful conversation partners. There has been significant psychiatric research on apathy, especially among people with severe illnesses such as Alzheimer's or Parkinson's disease. However, the research may have a broader application to all who are trying to make sense of apathy. One of the most commonly cited definitions describes apathy as a *lack of motivation* that "is not attributable to a diminished level of consciousness, an intellectual deficit, or emotional distress."[20] Other scholars tend to focus on the *lack of initiative* as the main characteristic of apathy: it is "an absence of responsiveness to stimuli as demonstrated by a lack of self-initiated action."[21] Here are the criteria used by various experts for checking if someone is experiencing apathy:

Lack of motivation relative to the patient's previous level of functioning or the standards of his or her age and culture, as indicated either by subjective account or observation by others. Presence, with lack of motivation, of at least one symptom belonging to each of the following three domains:

(1) Diminished goal-directed behavior:
    (a) lack of effort,
    (b) dependency on others to structure activity.

(2) Diminished goal-directed cognition:

---

20 Robert S. Marin, "Differential Diagnosis and Classification of Apathy," *American Journal of Psychiatry* 147, no. 1 (1990): 22.
21 Robert van Reekum et al., "Apathy: Why Care?" *The Journal of Neuropsychiatry and Clinical Neurosciences* 17 (2005): 8.

(a) lack of interest in learning new things or in new experiences,
(b) lack of concern about one's personal problems.

(3) Diminished emotion:
(a) unchanging affect,
(b) lack of emotional responsivity to positive or negative events.

The symptoms cause clinically significant distress or impairment in social, occupational, or other important areas of functioning.[22]

In simpler terms, this is saying that if a patient feels less motivated than those around him regarding the same important things, then he might be on the road to apathy. If the lack of motivation is accompanied by a lack of effort, lack of interest in learning, or lack of emotion, then the patient might be clinically diagnosed with a real condition. These symptoms are often diagnosed through a test known as the Apathy Evaluation Scale, in which patients (and clinicians) respond to the following eighteen statements with a rating from 1 to 4—not at all, slightly, somewhat, or a lot (feel free to evaluate yourself):

1. I am interested in things.
2. I get things done during the day.
3. Getting things started on my own is important to me.

22 Adapted from Sergio E. Starkstein et al., "Syndromic Validity of Apathy in Alzheimer's Disease," *American Journal of Psychiatry* 158 (2001): 876.

4. I am interested in having new experiences.

5. I am interested in learning new things.

6. I put little effort into anything.

7. I approach life with intensity.

8. Seeing a job through to the end is important to me.

9. I spend time doing things that interest me.

10. Someone has to tell me what to do each day.

11. I am less concerned about my problems than I should be.

12. I have friends.

13. Getting together with friends is important to me.

14. When something good happens, I get excited.

15. I have an accurate understanding of my problems.

16. Getting things done during the day is important to me.

17. I have initiative.

18. I have motivation.[23]

The patient's score is then assessed in various categories—initiative, emotions, interest—to see if he or she is, in fact, apathetic. Low scores point in the direction of apathy.

It may seem strange to attach all this technical jargon to something that seems so intuitive. This is why some patients simply report apathy as "the get up and go that got up and went" or "the spark is missing."[24] These phrases do a great job articulating a feeling many of us share. However, the value of clinical precision is that, as we get better at defining the ailment, we are better positioned to deal with it. For instance, apathy (as we'll see later)

---

23 Adapted from Robert S. Marin et al., "Reliability and Validity of the Apathy Evaluation Scale," *Psychiatry Research* 38 (1991): 150.

24 Van Reekum et al., "Apathy: Why Care?" 8.

overlaps with other conditions, such as depression. Knowing the differences is critical since the treatment of these may differ. Also, studies on apathy have been able to narrow down the various factors that contribute to it, such as environmental or biological factors. For example, immigrants or members of ethnic minorities sometimes adapt to differences in culture or language by becoming apathetic. The change in culture, or a feeling of being isolated within a culture, interferes with the pursuit of their values or goals, and apathy is just one way of coping or adapting to their environment.[25]

Studies also show that the kind of apathy we're concerned with is largely an *acquired* response to the world. It is not necessarily something you're born with and, therefore, destined to have for the rest of your life. Relatively healthy functioning people who are apathetic have lost interest in things—but only in *some* things. So, we are back to what I hinted at in the last chapter: the selectivity of apathy. In fact, one expert defines typical forms of apathy as "selective apathy."[26]

One final significant and relevant issue raised by researchers is whether to view apathy as a symptom of something else or as a unique syndrome. Generally speaking, a *symptom* is the pain or suffering that a patient reports. It often points to a more significant issue. A *syndrome*, however, is a group of symptoms that consistently occur together and characterize a particular illness.[27] Apathy, as basically a lack of motivation, should be treated as a symptom if this

---

25 Marin, "Differential Diagnosis," 24.

26 Marin, "Differential Diagnosis," 24.

27 See Robert S. Marin, "Apathy: A Neuropsychiatric Syndrome," *The Journal of Neuropsychiatry and Clinical Neurosciences* 3 (1991): 246.

lack is caused by some larger disturbance of mind or emotion. For example, apathy can be a symptom of depression and can be dealt with by treating the depression. On the other hand, apathy should be called a syndrome when the lack of motivation can't be attributed to some other impairment. My main concern in this book is not with the symptom but with the sickness, the syndrome. I want to solve the mystery of the "meh" that seems to have come out of nowhere. The psychiatric literature is helpful in showing that apathy is definable, diagnosable, and even treatable. It's a very real thing.

Apathy's Cousins

In attempting to distinguish between apathy as a symptom versus a syndrome, we highlight the basic truth that apathy *is* often closely related to other syndromes. Therein lies a challenge. One of the difficulties in defining and dealing with apathy is that there are several other sicknesses that resemble it, but are not identical. We've already spent time looking at acedia, but have only made fleeting references to some of apathy's other "cousins," what I'll call the three D's: depression, despondency, and dry spells. Proper treatment is married to proper diagnosis. So as our final conversation, let's get acquainted with these cousins so that we can spot true apathy when we see it and then deal with it accordingly.

Depression

Depression can take both severe and mild forms. Clinicians differentiate between major depression and what is called dysthymia. Major (or clinical) depression—my focus here—is a disorder in which someone experiences persistent feelings of sadness and a general sense of hopelessness. Physical symptoms, such as digestive issues, may accompany the emotional distress. To be diagnosed with major depression, someone must experience such symptoms as suicidal ideation, feelings of worthlessness, fatigue, and so forth for at least two weeks.[28]

More poetically, depression is described as a "stubborn darkness."[29] According to one writer, it is "a complete absence: absence of affect, absence of feeling, absence of response, absence of interest." The depressed are the "walking, waking dead."[30]

How do apathy and depression relate, then? While there is overlap, there is much that separates them, as the figure below shows:[31]

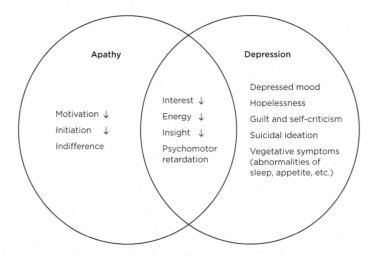

Fig. 2.1. Apathy and Depression

28 See APA, *DSM-5* (Washington, DC: American Psychological Association, 2013).

29 Edward T. Welch, *Depression: Looking Up from the Stubborn Darkness* (Greensboro, NC: New Growth, 2011).

30 Elizabeth Wurtzel, *Prozac Nation: Young and Depressed in America* (New York: Houghton Mifflin Harcourt, 2017), 2.

31 Junko Ishizaki and Masaru Mimura, "Dysthymia and Apathy: Diagnosis and Treatment," *Depression Research and Treatment* (2011): 1.

Both apathy and depression appear to have no discernible trigger; both often seem to come from nowhere. Yet, while some symptoms of apathy, such as a decrease in interest or energy, are also symptoms of depression, apathy may be present even when there are no clear signs of depression (e.g., hopelessness or depressed mood). On the other hand, those with major depression commonly experience apathy, too, but those who experience only minor depression may not experience any apathy.[32] Depression tends to be pervasive, taking over every formerly pleasurable part of life; apathy, as we have seen, is selective. Thus, apathy may be a symptom or sign of depression, but it may also be its own thing. Either way, it must be treated—and its treatment should be determined largely by whether it's a symptom or syndrome.

Despondency

While some writers translate the term *acedia* as "despondency" (and that is valid), I'd like to focus on despondency as a deep and persistent sense of discouragement, sadness, and helplessness that sometimes plagues even the most faithful believers. One writer, Martyn Lloyd-Jones, describes this condition as "spiritual depression." He draws on Psalm 42:5a, in which the psalmist cries out, "Why are you downcast, O my soul, / and why are you in turmoil within me?" Lloyd-Jones writes, "The fact remains that there are large numbers of Christian people who give the impression of being unhappy. They are cast down, their souls are 'disquieted within them.'"[33] The despondent person is sad,

---

32 Ishizaki and Mimura, "Dysthymia and Apathy," 4.
33 D. Martyn Lloyd-Jones, *Spiritual Depression: Its Causes and Its Cure* (Grand Rapids, MI: Eerdmans, 1965), 10.

perplexed, fearful, and overwhelmed. However, he or she is still engaged with God and pursuing him: "Hope in God!" (v. 5b), the psalmist tells himself.

In *The Pilgrim's Progress*, the protagonist, Christian, early in his journey finds himself slipping into the "Slough of Despond" (a slough is a swamp). After struggling for a while, he encounters a man named "Help," who assists him out of the slough. As he does so, he provides an apt description of the swamp and of despondency itself. "As the sinner is awakened about his lost condition," he observes, "there ariseth in his soul many fears, and doubts, and discouraging apprehensions which all of them get together, and settle in this place."[34] Notice that the swamp is filled with fears, doubts, and discouragements, but it mainly burdens those who are awakened to their sin and are on their way to the Celestial City.

While both apathy and despondency are perplexing and may inhibit action, despondency is not the deadening of emotion, but rather the deep experience of emotion—even overwhelming emotion. The despondent are overwhelmed but may still try to engage with God, while the apathetic find it difficult to do even that.

Now, we don't want to draw overly strict distinctions between these conditions, yet we do want to note their subtle differences. Lack of feeling or lack of initiative are quite different than dejection or perplexity. In despondency, God feels distant because of circumstances, doubts, or discouragements, while in apathy, we basically don't care where he is.

34 John Bunyan, *The Pilgrim's Progress* (Ware: Wordsworth, 1996), 14.

Dry Spells

What do we make of those times when we experience an un-explainable dryness in our devotional lives? A. W. Tozer has a wonderful little essay entitled "Understanding Those Dry Spells," which he opens by saying, "Probably nothing else bothers the earnest Christian quite so much as the problem of those dry spells that come to him occasionally, no matter how faithfully he tries to obey God and walk in the light. He can never predict them and he cannot explain them. And there lies his difficulty."[35]

Our first instinct during dry times, when we're not feeling God especially closely, is to ask whether there is some sin in our lives that is keeping God far from us. While this is probably a decent instinct for the faithful Christian, it usually doesn't scratch the itch. We find ourselves feeling the aridity of our day-to-day experience of God even after we've examined our hearts and lives. God's presence seems far from us, and we don't feel a great deal of joy.

Yet, Tozer remarks that these spiritual deserts are a gift of God—for we would never develop deep faith without these wilderness seasons. "If we never came down from the mount of blessing we might easily come to trust in our own delights rather than in the unshakeable character of God."[36]

Tozer is highlighting something similar to what has come to be known as the "dark night of the soul," a concept popularized by a monk named John of the Cross, but commonly understood throughout all ages of the church. In John's version, he argues that God takes believers through two dark nights—those of the

35 A. W. Tozer, *The Root of the Righteous* (Harrisburg, PA: Christian Publications, 1955), 126.
36 Tozer, *Root of the Righteous*, 128.

senses and of the spirit. The whole aim is to wean Christians from an overreliance on anything other than God. During the dark night of the senses, God purifies us from idols of possessions, relationships, or feelings, and even removes the former sense of enjoyment we had in performing spiritual practices. In the dark night of the spirit, God seeks to purge us of false beliefs and false images of him. He removes spiritual comforts and allows the soul to feel abandoned. All this is meant to draw the believer to trust in God apart from feelings and any other crutches.[37] The dark night is a wisely orchestrated plan by a loving Father who cares to bring his children to maturity.

It is possible that apathy has a divinely initiated purpose behind it; God could be stripping us of reliance on our feelings. However, unlike apathy, dry spells do not necessarily incline a person to withdraw from God (though they might). Dry spells are seasons of real sadness, but also of longing for more. With apathy, there is a deeper sense that things are messed up, but there is no palpable longing for more of anything meaningful. In dry spells, God actively removes the *feeling* of his presence for our good. Apathy is more perplexing; it *may* result from sin in our lives, and, if left unchecked, can lead to a slow drift away from God.

The Vandalism of Shalom

What, then, is apathy? Who exactly is this enemy that stands against us? It should be clear that we are miles (and hundreds of years) away from the ancient virtue of *apatheia*. Our apathy is the exact opposite of the apathy our forebears lauded. Ours is loveless;

37 See Bruce Demarest, *Seasons of the Soul: Stages of Spiritual Development* (Downers Grove, IL: InterVarsity Press, 2009), 87–90, for a helpful summary of John's teaching.

theirs was defined by love. Ours denounces self-discipline; theirs required it. That being the case, what can we learn from our various other conversations throughout this chapter?

It would appear from our dialogue with its cousins that apathy is neither deep depression, despair, nor discouragement. It is not the mysterious movement of the faithful Christian groping in the darkness toward God. Rather, it is a middling posture that flits between confusion and disengagement. It bears a family resemblance to its cousins but lacks their depth of feeling. Apathy, as the psychological literature has made us aware, is at root a deficit in motivation, effort, interest, initiative, and desire toward things we formerly found meaningful. It is a psychological disorder, possibly not of the same magnitude as clinical depression, but still debilitating in its own way.

The concept of acedia provided the most robust and true-to-experience description of the kind of apathy we're concerned about—apathy toward the things of God. Let's remind ourselves of the various ways acedia was described by our monastic friends:

- hatred of industry (or productivity)
- restlessness
- laziness in prayer
- lack of discipline
- lack of Bible reading
- relaxation (nondiligence) of soul
- discontentment
- selective laziness
- lack of perseverance
- lack of love for/joy in God

Acedia merely describes the blahness we feel toward the things of the Spirit; it is a name for the spiritual dimension of apathy. Yet, if we are to have a full-orbed definition of apathy, we must also attend to its psychological and emotional dimensions. So here's my attempt at a definition:

Apathy is a psychological and spiritual sickness in which we experience a prolonged dampening of motivation, effort, and emotion, as well as a resistance to the things that would bring flourishing in ourselves and others. It is a sin that expresses itself as restlessness, aimlessness, laziness, and joylessness toward the things of God.

In this definition, I've sought to weave together the most salient features of everyday apathy: its spiritual and psychological aspects, its lethargy, and its selectivity. But note that I have described it as a sickness. It is not just a part of highly evolved adult behavior, something like being too cool to care. It is an illness.

But is it *really* a sin? To some, it seems harsh to label apathy a sin. However, I wonder if our discomfort over the label arises from our lack of a careful and biblical understanding of the nature of sin. We have to ask: Is sin a *contagion* to be cleansed, a *captor* from which we need release, or a *crime* to be pardoned? The answer: yes, yes, and yes. Scripture speaks of sin as a sickness that spreads to all people from its source in Adam (Rom. 5:12) and remains alive in us, producing all kinds of evil (7:8; 20). It also declares that we were slaves to sin, needing release from captivity (John 8:34–36; Rom. 6:6). Finally, sin is described as lawlessness (1 John 3:4), bringing condemnation (Rom. 5:18; 6:23), and requiring propitiation (3:23–25; 1 John 2:2).

Cornelius Plantinga describes sin as the "vandalism" of sha-lom. Shalom, biblically speaking, means "universal flourishing, wholeness, and delight"—the way things were meant to be. We violate shalom when we turn against the very good order God has established. We subvert it when we live in such a way that under-mines our and others' wellbeing and joy. And because shalom is ultimately about our relationship to our Maker, its vandalization is directed toward God. As Plantinga writes, "Sin is not only the breaking of law but also the breaking of covenant with one's savior. Sin is the smearing of a relationship, the grieving of one's divine parent and benefactor, a betrayal of the partner to whom one is joined by a holy bond." This smearing happens through our actions as well as our attitudes.[38]

In light of the multifaceted nature of sin, can we call apathy a sin? Unfortunately, yes. Apathy is a sickness of the soul; it is a deformity of heart that needs healing. Apathy, as many of us experience it, is a form of bondage. We can't seem to lift ourselves out of it, finding ourselves regularly surrendering to its advances. Ultimately, apathy, as a refusal to love the one who is most love-able, is a moral and spiritual crime. It is a sin in the most basic sense. Its origins may be mysterious (we'll talk about that in the next chapter), but its orientation is not. It is a coldness to God and an indifference to the things that bring shalom—both of which need to be forgiven, conquered, and healed.

---

38 Cornelius Plantinga Jr., *Not the Way It's Supposed to Be: A Breviary of Sin* (Grand Rapids, MI: Eerdmans, 1996), 7–14.

We ought to grieve our apathy, but we do not grieve it as those who have no hope. God is with us and for us in our apathy. But before exploring God's cure for apathy, we'll take a look at some of the possible causes of our mystifying sickness.

Questions for Reflection

1. Even though you are far removed from a monastery, what aspects of the monks' experience of acedia can you identify with? Have you found helpful ways to combat it?

2. How do you respond to the idea that apathy is a sin? Does that sit well with you? Why or why not?

3

Everyone's Got a Story

Seven Deadly Causes of Apathy

HAVE YOU EVER SURPRISED yourself by how poorly you responded to a glance, a comment, or a conversation? Or have
you wondered why you seem to be more patient, empathetic,
or compassionate toward certain types of people than toward
others? In many instances, our life stories lie at the roots of our
responses. If you want to begin to understand my reactions,
responses, or general way of approaching life, get to know my
story.

For instance, here are some tidbits of my story that often inform
my perspective and, therefore, my responses:

- I was born in Nigeria but moved to North America as an
  infant. I grew up in Toronto, Canada.
- The neighborhood where I lived during my formative years
  was comprised of kids from families like mine, immigrants

from Turkey, South Korea, Japan, Greece, Poland, Germany, Norway, and China.

- As is the case for many immigrant families, our beginnings were meager economically.
- My parents were college educated. This, coupled with being an immigrant, placed pressure on me to succeed professionally.
- At eighteen, I became (at the time) the only Christian in my family of six.

Now, these plot points don't *determine* how I think or feel in every situation, but they certainly inform my thinking and feeling in some important conversations—conversations about culture, identity, work ethic, success, and immigration, to name a few. You see, our stories matter.

There is a branch of medicine known as *etiology*, which studies the causes of diseases. One college describes it as the study of the "backstory" of an illness. Etiology tries to figure out why a particular disease manifests in a particular person. Generally, the causes of diseases fall into three categories: intrinsic (originating from within), extrinsic (coming from external factors), and idiopathic (unknown).[1] Just as everybody has a story, every disease has a story (a history, a set of causes). To successfully treat an illness, we need to know its causes. The better the etiology, the better the treatment. And it is no different with apathy.

This chapter is an etiology of apathy. We are often bewildered about how we've become numb to doing evangelism, reading

---

1   "Etiology vs. Epidemiology: Important Concepts in Nursing," Regis College blog, https://online.regiscollege.edu/blog/.

our Bibles, praying, pursuing holiness, engaging in ministries of mercy, and so on. There really is a mysterious (or you can call it idiopathic) quality to apathy. Sometimes it feels as if it comes out of nowhere. Yet, the cause is not *all* mystery. Like other diseases, apathy has its own backstory in each person. My modest goal in this chapter is to uncover possible backstories, focusing on *some* of the "intrinsic" and "extrinsic" sources of our apathy. I want us to be able to identify our (possible) stories so that we can make sense of them and so that we might best apply the cure (chap. 4) and appropriate combat strategies (chap. 5). With that said, let's take a look at what I'm calling the *seven deadly causes of apathy.*

Backstory 1: Doubt

"*Je pense, donc je suis.*" This statement by René Descartes is one of the most famous in the history of Western philosophy. The translation, "I think, therefore I am," is a claim that valorizes doubt as the path to true knowledge. When we ruthlessly doubt everything, we find there is one thing we cannot doubt, and that is the fact that we are thinking when we doubt. Thus, doubt is the way to truth and life.

Even when it relates to our faith, some see doubt as constructive. George Macdonald writes, "A man may be haunted with doubts, and only grow thereby in faith. Doubts are the messengers of the Living One to the honest. They are the first knock at our door of things that are not yet, but have to be, understood."[2] Doubt is a repeatable rite of passage. There is no avoiding it on

2   *George MacDonald: An Anthology—365 Readings*, ed. C. S. Lewis (New York: Harper-Collins, 2001), 78.

the path to spiritual maturity. It is profoundly normal. As C. S. Lewis admits, "Now that I am a Christian I do have moods in which the whole thing looks very improbable. . . . This rebellion of your moods against your real self is going to come anyway."[3]

I have often struggled with doubt as a Christian—doubts about God's existence, about where I will go when I die, and about Jesus's uniqueness. And when it comes to *my* Christian life, very few things can take the wind out of my spiritual sails like doubt. So, while I am consoled somewhat by the fact that doubts are normal and potentially formative, they still feel like what Lewis calls an emotional "blitz" on my belief.

We might split doubt into three categories. First, there is factual or philosophical doubt, which has to do with questions regarding history, evidence, or more abstract questions concerning God's existence or the problem of evil. The second and most common category is emotional doubt. This mode of doubt expresses itself in repeated "what if" or "why" questions, even after sufficient intellectual responses may have been given. This is often where my doubt resides, focusing on the possibility that I could in some way have been misled. Third, volitional doubt is essentially a retreat from theological, philosophical, or any potentially helpful discussion altogether. The doubting person is deadened inside and, because of hurt, exhaustion, or anger at God, lacks motivation to engage in his or her Christian life. Sometimes doubt moves from philosophical to emotional to volitional if left unaddressed at each stage. Unsatisfying intel-

3   C. S. Lewis, *Mere Christianity* (Glasgow: Collins, 1977), 121–22. He describes faith as the art of holding on to things you once thought reasonable, in spite of your changing moods.

lectual answers may lead to emotional questions; if emotional concerns persist for a long time, the doubter may grow bitter (volitional doubt). It appears most difficult to pull someone from this form of doubt.[4]

Whether doubt arises from our changing "moods" or from sincere intellectual questions, the effect is often the same: inaction, paralysis, spiritual limpness. Why pray, for example, if I doubt there is a God on the other end, or at least a God who cares? Os Guinness describes doubt as the mind's "suspension between faith and unbelief." He adds, "To believe is to be in one mind about accepting something as true; to disbelieve is to be in one mind about rejecting it; and to doubt is to waver somewhere in between the two, and thus to be in two minds."[5] Karl Barth calls doubt a "swaying and staggering between Yes and No."[6] The term *double-mindedness* is an excellent biblical category for doubt. It captures the idea of wavering between two opinions, or "standing in two boats," as a Chinese proverb describes it. But Guinness's enticing word *suspension* puts the finger on what doubt does to us. It suspends movement. It leaves us hanging. It causes an epic slowdown. Doubt takes us out at the kneecaps and can lead to permanent paralysis (i.e., unbelief) if left unattended.

A number of studies have probed the effect of religious doubt on the faithful. One such study surveyed 1,629 people from a variety of denominations, cultural backgrounds, and educational

4 Discussion summarized from Gary R. Habermas, "When Religious Doubt Grows Agonizing," *Christian Research Journal* 36, no. 2 (2013).

5 Os Guinness, "I Believe in Doubt," *Tabletalk* magazine, Jan. 1, 1992, https://www .ligonier.org/.

6 Karl Barth, *Evangelical Theology: An Introduction* (Grand Rapids, MI: Eerdmans, 1992), 124.

levels, both married and single, and coming from different parts of the United States. It consisted of 135 items and probed issues of religious doubt, religious practice, and mental health. The study found that religious doubt—in this case, arising from the problem of suffering and evil—had a negative impact on overall mental health, particularly expressing itself in the forms of depression, anxiety, paranoia, hostility, and obsessive-compulsive symptoms.[7] An earlier study of adults aged sixty-six years and older found that greater doubt about religion is associated with a decline in life satisfaction, self-esteem, and optimism. Religious doubt can even harm one's physical health (for example, causing negative sleep quality). Most of these effects are especially prevalent among younger populations, but decrease as people age or attain higher levels of education. The negative effects are also especially pronounced among clergy, who find themselves isolated and unable to bring their doubts to others. Not surprisingly, studies show that those with greater certainty in their beliefs have better mental and emotional health, likely because their faith enables them to process and cope with stressors.[8]

7 Kathleen Galek et al., "Religious Doubt and Mental Health across the Lifespan," *Journal of Adult Development* 14 (2007): 16–25. Throughout this chapter, I've assumed the complexity of trying to detangle apathy from its cousins. For example, since apathy can be a symptom of depression, identifying the sources of depression would be a critical step toward healing both depression and apathy.

8 See Neal Krause, "Religious Doubt and Psychological Well-Being: A Longitudinal Investigation," *Review of Religious Research* 47 (2006): 287–302; Neal Krause and Keith M. Wulff, "Religious Doubt and Health: Exploring the Potential Dark Side of Religion," *Sociology of Religion* 65 (2004): 35–56; Christopher Ellison et al., "Religious Resources, Spiritual Struggles, and Mental Health in a Nationwide Sample of PCUSA Clergy," *Pastoral Psychology* 59 (2010): 287–304; Christopher Ellison et al., "Religious Doubts and Sleep Quality: Findings from a Nationwide Study of Presbyterians," *Review of Religious Research* 53 (2011): 119–36; and Christopher Ellison, "Religious

The basic point is that the intuitive connection between doubt and apathy may have some support in the psychological and social scientific literature. Apathy is very likely to be one of the depressive symptoms arising from religious doubt. Doubt debilitates. It saps the pep in our step and locks our feet in cement. G. K. Chesterton gestures in this direction when he speaks of modernity's noble doubters: "In their doubts of miracles there was a faith in a fixed and godless fate; a deep and sincere faith in the incurable routine of the cosmos."[9] Here's the connection: doubt about God and the miraculous inclines one toward a sort of fatalism, a surrender to the unalterable forces of life. If whatever is going to happen will happen regardless of me, why even bother engaging? On top of this, when we persist in doubt, we toy dangerously with Friedrich Nietzsche's famous proposition that "God is dead"—killed by our unbelief, relegated to irrelevance.[10] Rather than empowering supermen who can now live out their lives with a sense of real self-determination, creeping unbelief leads to a world of meaninglessness. And a world lacking in meaning is a world for which it's difficult to get up in the morning.

Is doubt the backstory to your apathy? What unresolved questions do you have about God or your faith that keep you from engaging your spiritual life wholeheartedly?

Involvement and Subjective Well-Being," *Journal of Health and Social Behavior* 32 (1991): 80–99.

9   G. K. Chesterton, *Orthodoxy* (London: Bodley Head, 1957), 217.

10 Friedrich Nietzsche, *The Gay Science*, trans. Walter Kaufmann (New York: Vintage, 1974), 181–82.

Backstory 2: Grief

In the early days of the COVID-19 pandemic, the *Harvard Business Review* published an article entitled "That Discomfort You're Feeling Is Grief." In it, the author recounts a virtual meeting with fellow editors. As colleagues shared how they were feeling amid the pandemic, one used the surprising word *grief* to describe her feelings, prompting others (in their little videoconferencing boxes) to nod in approval. The shared, familiar feeling of blah was grief.

The article goes on in the form of an interview with David Kessler, an expert on grief. The interviewer asks, "Is it right to call some of what we're feeling grief?" Kessler responds, "Yes, and we're feeling a number of different griefs. We feel the world has changed, and it has. We know this is temporary, but it doesn't feel that way, and we realize things will be different. . . . The loss of normalcy; the fear of economic toll; the loss of connection. This is hitting us and we're grieving. Collectively. We are not used to this kind of collective grief in the air." Kessler goes on to speak about what he calls "anticipatory grief," which is tied to fear of the future, a dread of the unknown, and a perceived loss of safety.[11] Loss, fear, change, unpredictability—these are the sources of pandemic-induced grief.

Yet, we know these feelings are not unique to times of pandemic. Grief is a normal part of life because loss is normal. In the 1960s, Elisabeth Kübler-Ross developed the notion that people suffering loss often pass through five stages of grief: denial, anger,

---

11 Scott Berinato, "That Discomfort You're Feeling Is Grief," *Harvard Business Review*, March 23, 2020, https://hbr.org/.

bargaining, depression, and acceptance (the model has continually been refined and now contains a sixth stage—meaning). Denial has to do with going numb due to the shock of the loss. Anger is directed—rationally or irrationally—at anyone or anything involved in allowing the loss to occur. Bargaining has to do with "if only" statements and our desire to turn back the clock on our tragedy. Depression often accompanies grief, taking the form of deep sadness, emptiness, and a loss of purpose and motivation for living. Finally, acceptance is just that—accepting a new normal after the loss. It is finding new ways to reengage with life without denying the truth or pain of the loss.[12]

These stages—or, better, *states* or *symptoms*—of grief might be helpful in making some initial connections to apathy. Denial is numbness; bargaining keeps one anchored in the past, incapable of living well in the present; and depression often involves immobility. All of these effects are companions and even descriptors of apathy.

In July 1960, C. S. Lewis's wife, Joy Davidman, died of cancer. Devastated by the loss, Lewis took to journaling his experience of grief as a way of processing his pain. In one of his heart-wrenching reflections, he writes,

No one ever told me about the laziness of grief. Except at my job—where the machine seems to run on much as usual— I loathe the slightest effort. Not only writing but even reading a letter is too much. Even shaving. What does it matter now

---

12 For a good summary, see Elisabeth Kübler-Ross and David Kessler, *On Grief and Grieving: Finding the Meaning of Grief through the Five Stages of Loss* (New York: Scribner, 2005), 7–28.

whether my cheek is rough or smooth? They say an unhappy man wants distractions—something to take him out of himself. Only as a dog-tired man wants an extra blanket on a cold night; he'd rather lie there shivering than get up and find one.[13]

Grief is a motivation drain; it saps us of the drive to do both simple and meaningful tasks. The monk Evagrius personifies what he calls "sadness" as "one who dwells over loss"; he calls it "a kinsman to acedia."[14] Another monastic writer, John Cassian, views dejection as the source of acedia.[15] These insights accord with those of some psychologists, who identify apathy as a typical response to grief. It may be tied to the feeling of hopelessness (that nothing else matters); may be a means of self-preservation (grief hurts, so try not to care about anything); or may be the place a person lands when he or she has spent all emotion and simply feels empty.[16] Apathy can also be a sign that the process of grief has not run its course.[17]

Grief is about coping with loss. Gerald Sittser, an insightful guide on these issues, writes, "Loss creates a barren present, as if one were sailing on a vast sea of nothingness. Those who suffer loss

13 C. S. Lewis, *A Grief Observed* (New York: Bantam, 1976), 3–4.

14 *Evagrius of Pontus: The Greek Ascetic Corpus*, trans. Robert E. Sinkewicz, Oxford Early Christian Studies (Oxford: Oxford University Press, 2003)

15 John Cassian, *The Conferences of John Cassian* V.X, in *Nicene and Post-Nicene Fathers of the Christian Church*, Second Series, ed. Philip Schaff and Henry Wace (New York: Christian Literature Co., 1894), 11:343.

16 "Apathy: When No Feeling is the Hardest of All," Grief in Common blog, https://www.griefincommon.com/blog/.

17 Robert Taibbi, "Six Signs of Incomplete Grief," *Psychology Today*, June 7, 2017, https://www.psychologytoday.com/; and J. R. Averill, "Grief: Its Nature and Significance," *Psychological Bulletin* 70 (1968): 722, 727.

live suspended between a past for which they long and a future for which they hope."[18] There's that word *suspend* again. Like doubt, grief has the tendency to keep one suspended between two worlds and disengaged from the present. Losses can take many forms: disappointments with God; jobs lost or factories closing down; even gradual but real shifts in our cultural environment. These losses must be grieved, and part of that process may involve feelings of numbness or apathy. For example, a common experience among third-culture kids (TCKs)—those who have grown up in cultures different than their parents' home cultures—is the feeling of unresolved grief that sometimes leads to sadness, depression, and withdrawal. TCKs often experience the "hidden" losses of their familiar world, meaningful possessions, the comfortable and quirky patterns of life, relationships, status, and a tangible connection to their past.[19] These losses, as well, must be grieved because suppressed grief can lead from apathy to worse issues such as depression.

Is there something great or small you're currently grieving? Have you processed that grief before God or other people? Is this grief making you numb?

Backstory 3: Triviality

One of my favorite songs from a movie in recent years is the catchy tune "Everything Is Awesome" from *The Lego Movie*. We're first

---

18 Gerald L. Sittser, *A Grace Disguised: How the Soul Grows through Loss* (Grand Rapids, MI: Zondervan, 1995), 56.

19 David C. Pollock and Ruth E. Van Reken, *Third Culture Kids: Growing Up among Worlds*, rev. ed (Boston: Nicholas Brealey, 2009), 74–80.

introduced to it in the film as the lead character, Emmet, recites a litany of everyday events in his life he deems "awesome":

- Always use a turn signal.
- Park between the lines.
- Drop off dry cleaning before noon.
- Read the headlines.
- Don't forget to smile.
- Always root for the local sports team.
- Always return a compliment.
- Drink overpriced coffee.[20]

Emmet is so blind to the mundaneness of his life that he deems every lame experience as awesome. He has no real conception of what awesomeness really is. Driving the car, returning a compliment, or paying for overpriced coffee ("That's $37 dollars," says the barista. Emmet responds, "Awesome!")—all of these are equally awesome.

At the risk of taking all the fun out of a really fun song, I think Emmet and his little Lego world point to something about our own: we often lose touch with what is really meaningful. Everything is presented to us as momentous, worthy of comment, worthy of indulgence, so that our faculties become dull to the truly remarkable. We are numbed by triviality. If everything is awesome, everything ceases to be awesome.

In 2013, U.S. Sen. Marco Rubio, a Florida Republican, did the unspeakable: he took a sip of water while delivering a tele-

---

20 *The Lego Movie*, directed by Chris Miller and Phil Lord, Warner Bros., 2014.

vised rebuttal to President Barack Obama's State of the Union address. High unemployment, immigration, government spending, health care, the skyrocketing costs of higher education, and inner-city violence were deemed to be no more newsworthy than this purported gaffe by the senator. The media analyzed it to death. The late-night shows mocked it. *Saturday Night Live* parodied it. While Rubio's drink of water was less than suave, it's hard to see why it was treated as newsworthy, especially in a culture that claims to prize authenticity and "keeping things real." But we have been habituated to make a big stink about everything.

In the brilliant foreword to his equally brilliant book *Amusing Ourselves to Death*, Neil Postman contrasts the nightmarish visions of two important dystopian writers—George Orwell (*1984*) and Aldous Huxley (*Brave New World*)—and through them paints a chilling picture of the dangers we face today.

> What Orwell feared were those who would ban books. What Huxley feared was that there would be no reason to ban a book, for there would be no one who wanted to read one. Orwell feared those who would deprive us of information. Huxley feared those who would give us so much that we would be reduced to passivity and egoism. Orwell feared that the truth would be concealed from us. Huxley feared the truth would be drowned in a sea of irrelevance. Orwell feared we would become a captive culture. Huxley feared we would become a trivial culture . . .[21]

21 Neil Postman, *Amusing Ourselves to Death: Public Discourse in the Age of Show Business* (New York: Penguin, 2006), xix.

Postman is writing a lamentation about what happens to a culture that shifts from print to television as the predominant mode of conversation. In the tradition of Marshall McLuhan (who coined the famous saying "The medium is the message"), he argues that the form of our communication strongly limits what we are able and desirous to communicate. What becomes the important content of a culture are those bits that can be conveniently expressed through the dominant medium. For example, you would not use smoke signals to communicate a philosophical treatise. The form would restrict the content to only certain simple messages.[22] But what happens if the main medium is television, let alone the internet or social media? The inevitable outcome is the trivializing of communication; content is shaped so that what "works" on television or social media becomes what works overall. What often results is that big and small things, meaningful and meaningless events, are given equal billing based on how they "preach" on the preferred medium.

A sad but amusing example is offered in a chapter entitled "Now . . . This" in which Postman exposes the way television, especially TV news, stitches together the seminal and the fading. "There is no murder so brutal, no earthquake so devastating, no political blunder so costly . . . that it cannot be erased from our minds by a newscaster saying, 'Now . . . this.'" He goes on to say,

In television's presentation of the "news of the day," we may see the "Now . . . this" mode of discourse in its boldest and

22 Postman, *Amusing Ourselves to Death*, 6–7.

most embarrassing form. For there, we are presented not only with fragmented news but news without context, without consequences, without value, and therefore without essential seriousness; that is to say, news as pure entertainment.[23]

Comedienne Ellen Degeneres, in one of my favorite stand-up bits, captures this schizophrenic nature of television news. She shares how she often feels sorry for newscasters who have to flit back and forth between stories of tragedy and feel-good pieces: "There were no survivors. . . . And next, which candy bar helps you lose weight. . . . Still to come, there's an asteroid heading towards earth. . . . But first, where to find the cheesiest pizza in town!"[24]

In this context, where everything (marketable or entertaining) is awesome, what are we supposed to care about? Everything and nothing. The problem with making everything important is that everything can become *equally* important. It becomes harder and harder to *feel* the bigness of something that really is a big deal. We are pummeled by triviality until we finally wave the white flag and surrender to apathy. As Postman writes, "The public has adjusted to incoherence and been amused into indifference."[25] But again, the indifference is selective; it takes aim at meaningful things. The world may be going to hell, but Marco Rubio drank water!

If Postman's insights were true of the age of television, how much more so of our day of Instagram, Facebook, and Twitter, of Hulu, Netflix, and Prime? At a time when everything must

---

23 Postman, *Amusing Ourselves to Death*, 100.
24 Ellen Degeneres, *Ellen Degeneres: Here and Now* (New York: HBO Studios, 2005), DVD.
25 Postman, *Amusing Ourselves to Death*, 110–11.

be posted, liked, commented on, and retweeted, we are slowly conditioned to treat worthy things unworthily, or become more democratic and stop caring about everything equally.

Do you find yourself getting carried away by relatively insignificant things? Has the overwhelming amount of triviality flooding your inbox or feed moved you to stop caring altogether?

Backstory 4: Feelings of Inadequacy

A number of zeal-deflating feelings and thoughts fall under the broad category of "being overwhelmed." We may be overwhelmed by the difficulty of making a difference, by others' needs, or by our own shortcomings or lack of equipping. In the end, we are overwhelmed by the feeling of being inadequate and inconsequential. This results in a "Why bother?" approach to the important things of life.

We have to believe change is possible if we're ever going to take a stab at it. Sometimes circumstances can feel too daunting for us to want to try. A 2001 study in Germany found that Turkish immigrants were largely apathetic about German politics and political involvement. The study showed that the root of the immigrants' political apathy was the years of restrictions placed on immigrant voting and citizenship. In other words, a lack of access to political institutions erodes interest in politics, and that disinterest lingers even after access is finally granted. Similar studies have been carried out in the UK, with similar results. One group (native Germans or Brits) feels that its voice makes a difference, while the other group (immigrants) has little faith in the effectiveness of the political process to bring real change for its members.[26] Why waste time on something that's destined to fail? We often see this dynamic in our spiritual lives. If spiritual growth feels sluggish or nonexistent, even after repeated attempts on our part, we are tempted to believe it will never happen. And if it'll never happen, why bother?

It's one thing to be numbed by the trivial, but quite another to be numbed by the meaningful. Many of us have heard of what's known as compassion fatigue. It typically plagues those in helping professions (nurses, humanitarian workers, teachers, doctors) and is sometimes described as a feeling of helplessness in the face of society's many problems. People who are inclined to be especially empathetic can come to a place where they feel they can't commit any more time or energy to help others because they're overwhelmed or paralyzed by the seemingly endless needs around them. What often results is numbness, a loss of empathy, emotional disconnection, and a decreased sense of purpose.[27] The feeling is: I've done so much, yet done so little. I'm not able to make a difference, so why bother?

What happens when we are overwhelmed by our own inadequacies, real or perceived? What happens to us when we look around and see others apparently firing on all cylinders while we're sputtering?

Christians rightfully have a sense of their inadequacy. Our hearts have been trained by truths like "All have sinned and fall short of the glory of God" (Rom. 3:23), "By grace you have

---

26 Claudia Diehl and Michael Blohm, "Apathy, Adaptation or Ethnic Mobilisation? On the Attitudes of a Politically Excluded Group," *Journal of Ethnic and Migration Studies* 27: 401–20.

27 "Compassion Fatigue," *Psychology Today*, https://www.psychologytoday.com.

been saved through faith. And this is not your own doing" (Eph. 2:8), and "We have this treasure in jars of clay, to show that the surpassing power belongs to God and not to us" (2 Cor. 4:7). We are fragile, unimpressive clay pots; apart from God's kindness and power, we could not move a single inch toward Christlikeness. However, this kind of feeling of inadequacy is not inconsistent with diligence and optimism about spiritual growth. The apostle Paul writes, "[God's] grace toward me was not in vain. On the contrary, *I worked harder* than any of them, though it was not I, but the grace of God that is with me" (1 Cor. 15:10). When we acknowledge weakness, God's power is most present to us.

Yet, there is a way of feeling inadequate that can choke us. In a chapter provocatively titled "Compare Yourself to Who You Were Yesterday, Not to Who Someone Else Is Today," psychologist Jordan Peterson cautions against an overblown sense of our shortcomings. There is a critical voice inside of us, he writes, and it regularly condemns our less-than-stellar efforts and outcomes. It tells us that if we're not the best or awesome at something, it is foolishness to try. The voice has us compare ourselves to others—with discouraging results: "Who cares if you are the prime minister of Canada when someone else is the president of the United States?"[28] The voice tells us, "You're mediocre and lame; that's why nothing you do really makes a difference." Peterson warns against this voice; it is not the voice of wisdom. His advice:

There will always be people better than you—that's a cliché of nihilism, like the phrase, *In a million years, who's going to know*

28 Jordan B. Peterson, *12 Rules for Life: An Antidote to Chaos* (Toronto: Random House Canada, 2018), 86.

the difference? The proper response to that statement is not, Well, then, everything is meaningless, It's, *Any idiot can choose a frame of time within which nothing matters.* Talking yourself into irrelevance is not a profound critique. . . . It's a cheap trick of the rational mind.[29]

Our unrestrained sense of inadequacy puts us into early retirement or, as Peterson puts it, talks us into irrelevance. We deem ourselves inconsequential. This is just a fancy way of saying we simply don't matter. Those who are overwhelmed feel inconsequential, as if they're not able to make a real difference. And if we and our actions are ultimately irrelevant, why bother?

Do you repeatedly size yourself up against other people, or even your own ideals, and come up lacking? If so, does this often discourage you from doing meaningful things? Have you fallen prey to a "Why bother?" mentality in your life?

Backstory 5: Lack of Discipline

While a complex of psychological, emotional, and cultural factors may contribute to our apathy, sometimes its root is less than complicated. Our blahness toward our spiritual lives may simply be the result of a lack of discipline and diligence in the very basics of our faith. We stoke our fires for certain things while we let the embers die out in our spiritual lives.

For example, a 2019 global study found that the average gamer (someone who plays an online game at least once a week) spends

29 Peterson, *12 Rules for Life*, 87.

over seven hours a week in this activity. That's a surprisingly low number, but notice the focus is on *online* games. Another study shows that 56 percent of kids between thirteen and seventeen years of age spend at least 2.5 hours a day on video games, while 66 percent of those eight to twelve years of age spend at least two hours. Add to this the fact that children spend seven hours per day interacting with media. On top of this, the average American watches 2.8 hours of television per day (19.6 hours per week), while those fifteen to forty-four years of age read less than ten minutes per day.[30] A youth pastor friend recently shared that it was not unheard of for students to spend seven hours a day on TikTok.

No one is disparaging leisure, TV, or gaming *per se*, yet the mathematics of spiritual impotence is simple:

buckets of time looking at screens + almost no time in spiritual disciplines = meh

Wilhelmus à Brakel, a seventeenth-century Dutch Reformed theologian, cautions against sluggishness, viewing it as "the fountain of all manner of sin, vain thoughts, fornication (2 Sam. 11:2), backbiting (Rom 1:30), unrighteousness, and despair." He exhorts, "Therefore, be fearful of laziness. He who is lazy in temporal matters will be lazy in spiritual matters, and he who is diligent in spiritual matters will be diligent in temporal matters."[31] An overarching lack

---

30 Kevin Anderton, "Research Report Shows How Much Time We Spend Gaming," *Forbes*, March 21, 2019, https://www.forbes.com/; "American Time Use Survey Summary," U.S. Bureau of Labor Statistics, June 25, 2020, https://www.bls.gov/; and "Video Games," Center on Media and Child Health, https://digitalwellnesslab.org/.

31 Wilhelmus à Brakel, *The Christian's Reasonable Service*, vol. 4, trans. Bartel Elshout, ed. Joel R. Beeke (Grand Rapids, MI: Reformation Heritage Books, 1995), 109.

of discipline inevitably infects our walk with God. Our thinking ("vain thoughts") and feeling ("despair") about the things of heaven become misshapen. The apostle Paul writes in Romans 8:5–7,

> For those who live according to the flesh set their minds on the things of the flesh, but those who live according to the Spirit set their minds on the things of the Spirit. For to set the mind on the flesh is death, but to set the mind on the Spirit is life and peace. For the mind that is set on the flesh is hostile to God, for it does not submit to God's law; indeed, it cannot.

The vibrancy of our spiritual lives has everything to do with what our minds are set upon. If our minds are regularly set on the things of the Spirit, we will experience abundant life and peace. However, if our minds are set on the things of the flesh, we will experience an inner hostility toward God. Paul is not talking merely about our thinking (though he is), but also about what we desire and how our lives are directed toward what we desire. The compound word *mindset* captures well what he is saying here.[32] A lazy, undisciplined, misdirected mindset leads to death, even the slow death characterized by the disordered nonaffections of apathy.

It sometimes seems as if we have lost all faith in the power of a disciplined life. We don't believe change is possible, or we believe that change comes only from "out of nowhere" or in some cataclysmic event. It can feel too simplistic or formulaic to assume that our growth in love for God and neighbor has a *direct* correlation to the discipline and regularity of spiritual practices. "Read your Bible,

32 Kenneth Berding, *Walking in the Spirit* (Wheaton, IL: Crossway, 2011), 30–31.

pray every day, and you will grow, grow, grow; don't read your Bible and forget to pray, and you will shrink, shrink, shrink"—this is a simpleton's song, so we think. What about the psychological dimensions of growth? What about a theology of divine grace? Christian growth is complicated! Yes, Christian maturity may involve attending to a number of things, but we must trim branches as well as water roots. We don't do algebra by scrapping arithmetic. One funds the other; they work together. Dallas Willard, an influential thinker on spirituality, is correct when he claims,

> We can become like Christ by doing one thing—by following him in the overall style of life he chose for himself. If we have faith in Christ, we must believe that he knew how to live. We can, through faith and grace, become like Christ by practicing the types of activities he engaged in, by arranging our whole lives around the activities he himself practiced in order to remain constantly at home in the fellowship of his Father.[33]

What did Jesus do? He prayed, practiced solitude, studied and meditated on God's word, and regularly served others. Thus, the mathematics of growth is also quite simple:

set mind on things of the Spirit + practice the things Jesus did = life

If we want to solve the mystery of our spiritual blahness and expose our apathy backstory, we would do well to reflect on the following questions:

33 Dallas Willard, *The Spirit of the Disciplines: Understanding How God Changes Lives* (New York: HarperCollins, 1991), ix.

As you look back on your day or week, month or year, what have you set your mind on? Have you ruthlessly sought to set it on the things of the Spirit (i.e., things that nurture your spiritual life)?

Backstory 6: Fragility

Apathy is sometimes a coping mechanism, one strategy for managing distress. It can be an emotional retreat from disappointment, grief, pain, and threats—even perceived threats. Fortifying ourselves against apathy may involve building up resilience in the face of hardship. But therein lies one of our problems. Many of us, especially those in the younger generations, have not been encouraged toward resilience. Instead, we have been shielded from the very things that would strengthen us. In the process, we have become fragile.

Nassim Nicholas Taleb, a best-selling statistician, argues that it is not even mere resilience we need, but what he calls *antifragility*. He groups things into three categories. First, *fragile* things require protection because they are delicate and cannot heal themselves. Second, *robust* things resist shock and stay the same. Finally, *antifragile* things take adversity and stress and become better. "Some things benefit from shocks; they thrive and grow when exposed to volatility, randomness, disorder, and stressors and love adventure, risk, and uncertainty," Taleb writes. If uncertainties are certain, and hardships are our common lot, how we respond to them becomes the critical issue. He adds, "Wind extinguishes a candle and energizes fire. . . . *You want to be the fire and wish for the wind.*"[34] Avoidance produces candles unable to handle a puff of air; embracing difficulty encourages a raging fire.

---

34 Nassim Nicholas Taleb, *Antifragile: Things That Gain from Disorder* (New York: Random House, 2012), 3 (emphasis added).

Greg Lukianoff and Jonathan Haidt cite a study of peanut allergies in children. Beginning with a group of infants, the researchers had half of the parents expose their children to peanut products and the other half abstain from giving peanuts to their children. When the children were five, the researchers tested for the prevalence of peanut allergies among the two groups. They found that in the group exposed to peanuts, about 3 percent of children had developed allergies, while in the nonpeanut group, 17 percent of the children had developed allergies—more than five times the number of cases! The conclusion is simple: rather than weakening the children, exposure to threat strengthened them, while a lack of exposure weakened the other kids. This is the principle that underlies vaccines, namely, that exposure to harm (in small doses) results in a stronger immune system.[35]

Humans are largely antifragile beings. The more we lean into that truth, the more antifragile we become; the more we ignore it, the more fragile we will be. "What does not kill me makes me stronger," writes Nietzsche[36]—a true statement in many (but not all) cases. This sentiment is echoed by the German Reformer Martin Luther, who describes trial and struggle as one of three prerequisites for really knowing God. What he calls *Anfechtung* is a faith-filled internal battle instigated by suffering, injustice, and pain. According to the Reformer, it teaches us "not only

---

35 Greg Lukianoff and Jonathan Haidt, *The Coddling of the American Mind: How Good Intentions and Bad Ideas Are Setting Up a Generation for Failure* (New York: Penguin, 2018), 20–21.

36 Friedrich Nietzsche, *Twilight of the Idols*, trans. Richard Polt (Indianapolis: Hackett, 1997), 6.

to know and understand, but also to experience how right, how true, how sweet, how lovely, how mighty, how comforting God's Word is, wisdom beyond all wisdom."[37] Most important, Scripture itself encourages us that "suffering produces endurance, and endurance produces character, and character produces hope" (Rom. 5:3–4).

Let's try to see the connection between fragility and apathy. Research suggests that increased fragility is connected to increasing mental-health issues, especially depression and anxiety.[38] Our inability to handle threats and distress can lead to less-than-ideal coping responses. Remember, apathy is a coping mechanism meant to shield us from the possibility of getting hurt or disappointed. Those who have the fortitude to stand in the path of pain don't have to resort to apathy or disengagement as a survival strategy. Self-protection is the mother of apathy; resilience and antifragility are her archenemies, as Fig. 3.1 illustrates.

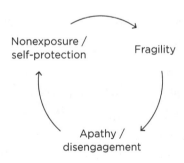

Fig. 3.1. Fragility and Apathy

37 Martin Luther, "Preface to the Wittenberg Edition of Luther's German Writings," *Luther's Works 34: Career of the Reformer IV*, ed. Lewis W. Spitz (Philadelphia: Muhlenberg, 1960), 287.

38 Lukianoff and Haidt, *Coddling of the American Mind*, chap. 7.

There is a vicious cycle: nonexposure to and nonacceptance of hardship lead to greater weakness, which then requires greater protection, which leads to further weakness, and so on. All the while, our self-protective bubble gets bigger and bigger, and pushes us further and further from the messy world of meaningful things. So, we are coddled into disengagement, indifference, and inaction. And disengagement feeds on itself, leading to greater degrees of apathy. Sadly, by shielding ourselves from threats—perceived or real—we also cut ourselves off from perseverance, character-building, and especially hope, the lack of which is a contributing cause of apathy (but the presence of which is an antidote).

Do you find yourself avoiding certain ministries, issues, or even people out of fear of getting hurt? Do you find yourself caring less and less about more and more things?

Backstory 7: Lack of Purpose

In the last chapter, we saw that listlessness and purposelessness are key features of acedia or spiritual apathy. We also saw earlier that doubt can lead to a world where everything ultimately loses meaning and purpose. Yet, a sense of purpose inspires us to meaningful, sustained action in life.

As I mentioned in the first chapter, during my years doing full-time campus ministry, I regularly struggled to find the motivation to do personal evangelism. My work required that I regularly begin spiritual conversations with strangers and take students involved in the ministry along with me for training. I knew nonbelieving students needed to hear the gospel, and

I knew Christian students needed to learn how to share their faith. Yet, I woke up many mornings wishing I didn't have to do it. Admittedly, some of this was nothing but fear. The prospect that a non-Christian would be rude or antagonistic scared me. However, at other times, the issue wasn't fear. I was simply not gripped by what I was doing.

Then, midway through my ministry years, I was exposed to the ministry of John Piper, who regularly beat the drum of God's glory being the main goal of human life. At that time, I caught a vision for evangelism also being about the glory of God—about the Father and Son getting glory by my simple act of telling people about their wonderful work of redemption, regardless of how those people responded. For some reason, that vision captured me, and for a span of a few years, it fueled my willingness to do the uncomfortable and share my faith.

Those years have been branded in my mind as an example of how a sense of purpose motivates. For each of us, the particular purpose that grips us will be different. But purpose inspires. Simon Sinek, in his bestselling leadership book *Start with Why*, tries to get to the heart of what motivates long-term growth and significant movement in organizations and individuals. According to Sinek, all corporations know *what* they do or produce. Most can articulate *how* they do it. However, many organizations are unclear as to *why* they do what they do. Yet, it is the *why* that inspires. He presents Apple as a prime example of a company that knows how to motivate with *why*. Rather than presenting the *what* of their products, Apple has figured out how to move customers because of its remarkable clarity regarding the *why*. Slogans such as "Think different" or "1,000 songs in your pocket" connect Apple's products (and customers) to a larger purpose and give reasons for consumers to choose Apple phones or tablets over comparable products.[39]

We all need purpose—young and old alike. Parenting expert Kathy Koch speaks of purpose as being one of the five core needs of children that must be met if meaningful change is to happen in their lives. "If children don't believe they were created on purpose with purpose to fulfill," she writes, "they won't be interested in improving skills or achieving mastery." She adds, "Without purpose and a vision for their tomorrows, they think they don't need to be good at anything. . . . Reasons they're alive can provide the motivation they need to take risks and persevere when things are challenging."[40] In other words, passion for growth dies when there is no sense of purpose. The mantra of the purposeless is "Why bother?"

After drowning (and drowning us) for twelve chapters in the apparent meaninglessness of life, the writer of Ecclesiastes jolts us out of indifference and despair with a crystal-clear life purpose statement: "Fear God and keep his commandments, for this is the whole duty of man" (Eccles. 12:13). He is saying that there is a focus that can clear the fog, a purpose that can reignite passion. But if we lose sight of it, we may find ourselves growing numb and immobilized, repeating in our hearts the refrain "Vanity of vanities, all is vanity" (1:2). Apathy feeds on aimlessness.

---

39 Simon Sinek, *Start with Why: How Great Leaders Inspire Everyone to Take Action* (New York: Portfolio/Penguin, 2009), 37–51.

40 Kathy Koch, *Start with the Heart: How to Motivate Your Kids to Be Compassionate, Responsible, and Brave (Even When You're Not Around)* (Chicago: Moody, 2019), 96.

Are you finding it difficult to answer the why *question for your life? Do your daily activities feel directionless, as if you're being carried by the winds of the day?*

We Wrestle against Flesh and Spirits

So, what's your story? Is it doubt, grief, or the feeling that you've been suffocated by triviality? Does your story include feelings of inadequacy, a lack of discipline, fragility, or a diminishing sense of purpose? Our apathy is likely to involve a combination of these and other backstories, and one person's set of causes will differ from another.

Yet, amid all the variety and complexity of our apathy stories, the common element is that our chief enemies are spiritual. In fact, every cause of apathy is spiritual in at least two senses. First, lurking behind the scenes there is a real enemy—the evil one—who relishes our apathy and loves to capitalize on the stuff going on inside and outside of us. He seeks to afflict us with some of the very causes we've uncovered. So, while we are trying to understand these particular causes of apathy from a down-to-earth perspective, I don't want us to lose sight of the spiritual arena in which we live and fight (Eph. 6:12).

Second, we are also at war with ourselves. What the Bible calls our *flesh*—that old, spiritually dead part of us—is prone to being dragged down. There is a real battle raging between our new self, which is created to be like Christ, and our old self, which would be perfectly content living apathetically (Col. 3:9–10).

To use the language described at the beginning of the chapter, there are both extrinsic and intrinsic spiritual forces permeating and exacerbating our apathy. "The devil made me do it!" is a partial truth for the Christian. It is true in the sense that the evil one seeks to steal, kill, and destroy, even if he does it through the subtle means of encouraging apathy through doubt, triviality, or false notions of ourselves. But it is a *partial* truth. We are responsible actors. We have to look apathy squarely in the face and be willing to wrestle it down. Part of that wrestling involves identifying its particular backstories in our lives. It may involve counseling, self-denial, and brutal honesty; discipline, inner strength, and true repentance. This fight may require no less than plucking out an eye or cutting off the hand that keeps us in the state of apathy.

Yet, what matters most in this fight is realizing that we're not alone in it. In fact, our partner (think tag-team wrestling) has already pinned our enemies to the mat.

Questions for Reflection

1. Which of the causes of apathy considered in this chapter do you think is the most common in your culture?

2. Which of the seven causes captures your (or your church's or friends') situation best? How, specifically, have you seen it on display?

3. Can you discern any common themes among these causes?

4

O Love That Wilt
Not Let Me Go

The Cure for Apathy

ONE OF THE MOST ENDURING and endearing English-language hymns of all time was written in about five minutes. "O Love That Wilt Not Let Me Go" is a masterpiece penned by George Matheson, a Scottish minister. Matheson was a gifted preacher, theologian, songwriter, and prolific author, having once been invited by Queen Victoria to preach a sermon (which she later had printed). He was also blind, having lost most of his eyesight by his late teen years. He never married, but lived with his sister, who took care of him and aided in his ministry. The verses of Matheson's most famous hymn are familiar to many:

O Love that wilt not let me go,
I rest my weary soul in Thee:

I give Thee back the life I owe,
That in Thine ocean depths its flow
May richer, fuller be.

O Light that followest all my way,
I yield my flickering torch to Thee:
My heart restores its borrowed ray,
That in Thy sunshine's blaze its day
May brighter, fairer be.

O Joy that seekest me through pain,
I cannot close my heart to Thee:
I trace the rainbow through the rain,
And feel the promise is not vain
That morn shall tearless be.

O Cross that liftest up my head,
I dare not ask to fly from Thee:
I lay in dust life's glory dead,
And from the ground there blossoms red
Life that shall endless be.[1]

This song has brought much joy to many, but if you read closely, you can see that it came from a place of hardship. Notice, for example, the beginning of the third stanza: "O Joy that seekest me through pain . . ." Matheson himself leaves a brief account about how the hymn originated:

---

1   "O Love That Wilt Not Let Me Go" by George Matheson, 1892.

My hymn was composed in the manse [minister's house] of Innellan on the evening of June 6th, 1882. I was at the time alone. It was the day of my sister's marriage, and the rest of the family were staying overnight in Glasgow. Something happened to me, which was known only to myself, and which caused me the most severe mental suffering. The hymn was the fruit of that suffering. It was the quickest bit of work I ever did in my life. I had the impression rather of having it dictated to me by some inward voice than of working it out myself. I am quite sure that the whole work was completed in five minutes, and equally sure that it never received at my hands any retouching or correction.

There is a popular (though never proven) belief that Matheson's "severe mental suffering" came as a result of his fiancée leaving him because she couldn't handle the prospect of being married to a blind man.[2] Perhaps his grief was compounded by the bittersweetness of his sister's wedding.

Regardless of the specific hardship, what's most striking about this song written by this blind and hurting minister is how he comforts himself. Matheson begins each stanza with the truth that God—as love, light, joy, and cross—holds on, guides, seeks, and lifts up. This is what Matheson puts in the foreground. This is where his hope lies.

This is where *our* hope lies.

What does God have to say to those who have a hard time caring about what he says about anything? Is the gospel good news to the apathetic? Matheson offers real help. Nothing describes the

2   This account is recorded in Kenneth W. Osbeck, *101 Hymn Stories: The Inspiring True Stories behind 101 Favorite Hymns* (Grand Rapids, MI: Kregel, 1982), 189–90.

apathetic person better than the words "weary soul" and "flickering torch." Yet, Matheson encourages us that God is love that won't let us go and light that reignites the dimming torches of our affections. This blind minister points us to the cure for the spiritually dumb and numb. God is the answer. The gospel is the remedy.

In this chapter, we'll explore how God addresses apathy and how understanding his work is pivotal for our ongoing battle with it. We'll first look at how the gospel is the cure for apathy, which (as we saw in chapter 2) is a form of sickness, bondage, and lawlessness. We'll then reflect on how God addresses the seven deadly causes of apathy discussed in the previous chapter.

The Greatest Drama Ever Staged

The gospel is a drama in which God is the lead actor. It is an announcement of what God has done in Christ and in the Spirit. The novelist and Christian apologist Dorothy Sayers calls it "the greatest drama ever staged." We find this drama throughout the pages of Scripture, and it centers on one man—Jesus of Nazareth. Sayers outlines this story (I give you only a snippet of her breathtaking summary):

> Jesus Bar-Joseph, the carpenter of Nazareth, was in fact and in truth, and in the most exact and literal sense of the words, the God *"by whom all things were made."* . . . He was in every respect a genuine living man. He was not merely a man so good as to be "like God"—He *was* God.
>
> Now, this is not just a pious commonplace; it is not commonplace at all. For what it means is this, among other things: that for whatever reason God chose to make man as he is—limited

and suffering and subject to sorrows and death—He [God] had the honesty and the courage to take His own medicine. Whatever game He is playing with His creation, He has kept His own rules and played fair. He can exact nothing from man that He has not exacted from Himself. He has Himself gone through the whole of human experience, from the trivial irritations of family life and the cramping restrictions of hard work and lack of money to the worst horrors of pain and humiliation, defeat, despair, and death. When He was a man, He played the man. He was born in poverty and died in disgrace and thought it well worthwhile.

After outlining other stunning features of Jesus's life—his healings, driving out of merchants from the temple, conflicts with leaders, love for the broken, and bodily resurrection—Sayers concludes,

Now, we may call that doctrine exhilarating or we may call it devastating; we may call it Revelation or we may call it rubbish; but if we call it dull, then words have no meaning at all. That God should play the tyrant over man is a dismal story of unrelieved oppression; that man should play the tyrant over man is the usual dreary record of human futility; but that man should play the tyrant over God and find Him a better man than himself is an astonishing drama indeed. Any journalist, hearing of it for the first time, would recognize it as News; those who did hear it for the first time actually called it News, and good news at that; though we are apt to forget that the word *Gospel* ever meant anything so Sensational.[3]

---

3   Dorothy L. Sayers, *Creed or Chaos? Why Christians Must Choose Either Dogma or Disaster* (Manchester: Sophia Institute, 1999), chap. 1.

This drama is not exhilarating or sensational because we are gifted supporting actors, and neither is it good news about something that we do, bring, enact, or fulfill. This is a vital point to make as we think about the cure for apathy. Apathy, like every other human deficiency, needs to be put into its proper context, and that context is the story of *God's* reconciling of the world in Christ (2 Cor. 5:19), of *him* making us a "new creation" (v. 17), of *Jesus's* overcoming of the world (John 16:33). We are not the cure to our apathy. God—Father, Son, and Spirit—is. It is what he did and continues to do on the stage of human history that makes all the difference.

In an earlier chapter, I spoke of apathy as one instance of the vandalism of shalom, as a sign of disorder in the soul and in God's good world. If the gospel is really good news, it speaks to and somehow solves this disruption of shalom. So, let's spend a few moments revisiting parts of this great drama of the gospel and touching on how God has acted as conqueror, healer, and forgiving judge, restoring shalom and even addressing our apathy.

Apathy Conquered

The gospel is the story of God's undying commitment to his *enslaved* creation. Scripture speaks of creation as in "bondage to corruption" and awaiting the day of its liberation. The centerpiece of that slavery-liberation narrative is humanity. When God's people are made free from slavery to sin and decay, creation will follow suit (Rom. 8:20–23). This passage assumes what other passages in the New Testament make explicit: humanity is in slavery to sin and Satan, and is therefore in need of rescue. In our natural state, we are captives in a prisoner of war camp, forced to do the bidding of our captors, longing for release.

This truth is captured time and again in the Gospels. In one of Jesus's many Sabbath controversies, he heals a woman who has been disabled for eighteen years. When confronted for healing on the Sabbath, Jesus responds, "Ought not this woman, a daughter of Abraham whom Satan bound for eighteen years, be loosed from this bond on the Sabbath day?" (Luke 13:16). Notice two things. First, Jesus attributes this crippling illness to Satan and calls it a form of bondage. Second, he implies that his mission is about releasing people from spiritual bondage.

Yet, it's not just sickness and Satan by which we're bound. In another dispute with his adversaries, Jesus tells them that "everyone who practices sin is a slave to sin," but "if the Son sets you free, you will be free indeed" (John 8:34–36). In other words, those whom the Son has not set free are in captivity and slavery to sin. The life, ministry, death, and resurrection of Jesus culminate in his defeat of *our* sin and *our* death. Paul writes, "The sting of death is sin, and the power of sin is the law," which leads him to exclaim, "But thanks be to God, who gives us the victory through our Lord Jesus Christ" (1 Cor. 15:56–57). When seeking to explain why God became a man—why God wrote such an extravagant story—John Calvin writes, "It was [the Redeemer's] task to swallow up death. Who but the Life could do this? It was his task to conquer sin. Who but very Righteousness could do this? It was his task to rout the powers of world and air. Who but a power higher than world and air could do this?"[4] God sent Jesus into the world to disarm the power of sin and Satan. In fact, he put

---

4 John Calvin, *Institutes of the Christian Religion*, ed. John T. McNeill, trans. Ford Lewis Battles, The Library of Christian Classics, vols. 20–21 (Philadelphia: Westminster, 1960), 2.12.2.

them to shame by his dying and rising again (Col. 2:15). God has once for all "delivered us from the domain of darkness and transferred us to the kingdom of his beloved Son, in whom we have redemption, the forgiveness of sins" (1:13–14).

Those of us who have suffered under the curse of apathy know what it is to feel bound and helpless. We feel enslaved to an indifference that we can't shake. Yet, while we may feel powerless to free ourselves, the gospel truth is that we are already set free. Our hearts and hands are not bound in chains. In some profound sense, we are right now liberated from slavery to apathy, even though we may give in to it at times. Paul's command to "consider yourselves dead to sin and alive to God in Christ Jesus" (Rom. 6:11) is no less true when we talk about the sinful bondage of apathy. Christ doesn't disarm sin in the abstract; he triumphs over the specific things that we are actually enslaved to. And he is leading us in triumph, even during those seasons when we consider ourselves dead to everything and alive to nothing.

Apathy Healed

The gospel is the story of God's unfailing commitment to his *sick* creation. The motif of sinfulness requiring healing is common in God's constant tussling with Israel. In one of the most moving descriptions of the Messiah's ministry, Isaiah writes of Israel:

> Surely he has borne our griefs
>   and carried our sorrows;
> yet we esteemed him stricken,
>   smitten by God, and afflicted.
> But he was pierced for our transgressions;

he was crushed for our iniquities;
upon him was the chastisement that brought us peace,
    and with his wounds we are healed.
All we like sheep have gone astray;
    we have turned—every one—to his own way;
and the Lord has laid on him
    the iniquity of us all. (Isa. 53:4–6)

This suffering servant comes to bring wholeness and health to a people so sick they believe he suffers for his own sake. There is a wonderful exchange here: Jesus's physical (and emotional) wounding for our spiritual healing. The incurable wound that needs healing is sin, rebellion, hard-heartedness, waywardness. But the beating and killing of Jesus bring shalom.

Elsewhere in Isaiah, God speaks comfort to his wayward people:

Because of the iniquity of his unjust gain I was angry,
    I struck him; I hid my face and was angry,
        but he went on backsliding in the way of his own heart.
I have seen his ways, but I will heal him;
    I will lead him and restore comfort to him and his
        mourners,
    creating the fruit of the lips. (Isa. 57:17–19)

Unjust and backslidden hearts need healing. The good news God offers is that he will heal and restore wholeness to those who don't seem to care much about God and his ways. When questioned about why he is dining with notorious sinners, Jesus responds, "Those who are well have no need of a physician, but those who are sick. I have not come to call the righteous but sinners to repentance" (Luke 5:31–32). Jesus describes himself as a physician who's on mission to heal those who are sick and recognize that they're sick. The sickness here? Unrighteousness— a disability we ourselves can't rehabilitate.

In the first episode of *The Chosen*, a compelling TV series about Jesus's ministry, we see healing and sin powerfully intertwined. In the closing scene, Mary Magdalene, a woman troubled for a long time with evil spirits, encounters a stranger who shows an unusual interest in her. She tries to escape his attention, telling him repeatedly to leave her alone. But then the stranger calls her by name: "Mary!" Until then, she'd been known to others by the alias "Lilith." A conversation is sparked:

Stranger: "Mary of Magdala!"
Mary: "Who are you? How do you know my name?"
Stranger: "Thus says the Lord who created you and he who formed you, 'Fear not, for I have redeemed you. I have called you by name. You are mine.'"[5]

Then Jesus—still a stranger to Mary—stretches out both arms, gently takes her face in his hands, and embraces the sobbing woman. This notoriously unclean, possessed, evil sinner is healed.

This scene brings me to tears every time I watch it (and that's a lot of times). I'm well aware that this is likely not how it actually

5 *The Chosen*, season 1, episode 1, "The Shepherd," written and directed by Dallas Jenkins, featuring Aaron Himelstein, aired September 20, 2017.

unfolded in real life, but it is no less powerful. It puts flesh to the bare-bones accounts in the Gospels of how Jesus healed and, by doing so, transformed people's lives.

From this encounter onward, Mary's life is completely transformed (we see this in subsequent episodes of the series and in the Gospels themselves). She is not just relieved of demons, but is called by name, known by God, welcomed into his family, forgiven of all transgressions, and made into a new creation. Likewise, when Jesus comes into our world and heals us of sin and its effects, we experience the most radical reorientation of our lives. We are cured of estrangement from God; we are restored to spiritual health. Our former disabilities no longer define us. We shed false identities and become our truer selves. We are no longer Lilith, but Mary once again.

That Jesus heals messed-up people is no dull story. That the God of the universe knows sin-sick people by name is glorious news. The healings of Israel, "tax collectors and sinners," and Mary point to certain truths about our own healings. First, we know that only God heals. Second, we know that God desires to heal. Third, those who know Jesus Christ are already healed of sin and its rippling effects. Fourth, in light of these, we assume that he wants to keep us healthy.

For the apathetic, it might be comforting to know that although we were once dead and disinterested in the things of God, we were healed. Yet, now we find ourselves experiencing the sickness of indifference and disinterest. Hasn't Christ healed us? Are we doomed to struggle unsuccessfully all on our own? The God who healed us and turned us decisively from being bored with him is still with us and for us. By his wounds, inflicted by even the apathetic, we *are* healed—right now—and can continually be healed by God.

Apathy Forgiven

The gospel is the story of God's unending commitment to his *rebellious* creation. Sin is bondage and sickness, but it is also a violation of trust, a transgression against divine love, and lawlessness. Sin thumbs a nose at the covenant of love between God and his creatures. Thus, our greatest need is to be forgiven.

The Gospels' story of the paralytic is striking in this regard (Mark 2:1–12). Four friends bring a paralyzed man to Jesus. They are unable to get direct access to Jesus because of the crowds filling the house where the Lord is teaching. In desperation, they rip a hole through the roof and lower their friend down in Jesus's presence. And Jesus, pleased by their faith, gives something they are likely not expecting. Rather than healing their friend, he says to him, "Son, your sins are forgiven." Bizarre . . . and possibly disappointing. I'm sure they are thinking, "He needs to be healed of his paralysis." Yet, Jesus looks at this man and gives him something he needs far more than the ability to walk. He gives him the gift of restored fellowship with God that only comes when sins are pardoned. When he finally gets around to healing the man's physical ailments, he does so primarily to provide hard evidence that he has authority to forgive sins.

Jesus is on a mission to not leave God's people alienated from their source of life. Throughout his earthly ministry, he forgives the paralytic, the sinful woman who anoints his feet (Luke 7:47–48), and many others. After he returns to his Father, his disciples continue his ministry by regularly preaching about this aspect of his mission. For instance, here is a sampling from the book of Acts:

> God exalted him at his right hand as Leader and Savior, to give repentance to Israel and forgiveness of sins. (5:31)

> To him all the prophets bear witness that everyone who believes in him receives forgiveness of sins through his name. (10:43)

> Let it be known to you therefore, brothers, that through this man forgiveness of sins is proclaimed to you, and by him everyone who believes is freed from everything from which you could not be freed by the law of Moses. (13:38–39)

God has forgiven all our sin, canceling the record of debt we owe by "nailing it to the cross" (Col. 2:13–14). We *have been* forgiven. The work is complete. This is why Paul can comfort us by the truth that "there is therefore now no condemnation for those who are in Christ Jesus" (Rom. 8:1).

This is great news for the apathetic Christian. As a sin, apathy is unique and yet not unique. As a misdirection of our attention and affection, it is the same as many other sins. But as a passive-aggressive hostility to God, it is a strange bird. Apathy is not the hostility of a shaking fist but of a gaping yawn. And when you think about it, what hurts more, someone's anger or someone's indifference toward you? Yet, even in our indifference to spiritual things, our salvation does not hang by a thin thread. God says to us, "No condemnation, now or ever." You are not condemned, but forgiven because you are one with Christ. As theologian Karl Barth put it, Jesus is the "Judge judged in our place," and because of that we are free from God's wrath.[6] As free people, we don't have to live in fear, dreading the moment when God says, "Enough is enough!" and cuts us off.

All of this—redemption, healing, and forgiveness—is what the writer Philip Yancey once provocatively called the "atrocious mathematics of the gospel."[7] Think of the parable of the workmen in Matthew 20: some start work at six in the morning, some at five in the afternoon, yet all receive the same wages. The Johnny-come-latelies are welcomed in just the same way as the diligent, long-suffering workers. That's hardly a way to motivate people to work long and hard, hardly a way to stimulate persevering obedience to God. Yet, that is the scandal of God's grace and forgiveness. Many apathetic people know they're in a bad place; some feel nothing. The "atrocious" math is that we bring very little and get the world offered back to us in return. That's no dull story!

As a Man Thinketh

Why rehearse these scenes of the gospel story in a book about apathy? I do so because the gospel tells us about what's really real. The drama of God's commitment to his creation is the truest thing about our world and the truest thing about our lives. Yes, our struggle against apathy is real. Yes, our fight against indifference

---

6 Karl Barth, *Church Dogmatics IV.1: The Doctrine of Reconciliation, Study Edition* (London: T&T Clark, 2009), 204.

7 Philip Yancey, *What's So Amazing about Grace* (Grand Rapids, MI: Zondervan, 1997), 59–60.

is important. Yet, simply because something is real and important doesn't make it defining. We are not chiefly our weaknesses, struggles, or sins. We are set free, healed, forgiven—not to mention cleansed, adopted, and newly created. "All this is from God, who through Christ reconciled us to himself," as Paul reminds us (2 Cor. 5:18). By revisiting the gospel, we are trying to reposition ourselves—take the right posture—in our fight against apathy. We do this by regaining a proper Christian self-image. As theologian Anthony Hoekema puts it,

> It will be generally granted, I believe, that what someone thinks of himself has much to do with the kind of life he will live. A person who sees himself as inferior to others will probably do inferior work, whereas a person who believes himself to be more capable than others will probably do better work. *A man tends to live up to his self-image.*[8]

We rise to the level of whom we perceive ourselves to be. If we see ourselves as weak, displeasing to God, stuck, and powerless, that self-image will become a self-fulfilling prophecy.

Martin Luther speaks of "two kinds of righteousness," which he calls "alien" and "proper." Alien righteousness is another's righteousness—Christ's—granted to us by faith. Luther writes, "Therefore a man can with confidence boast in Christ and say: 'Mine are Christ's living, doing, and speaking, his suffering and dying, mine as much as if I had lived, done, spoken, suffered, and died as he did.'" He describes us as "one flesh" with Christ,

---

8 Anthony A. Hoekema, *A Christian Looks at Himself* (Grand Rapids, MI: Eerdmans, 1975), 14 (emphasis added).

sharing all things in common with him.[9] The second kind—proper righteousness—refers to our life of good works, devotion, and love for neighbor. But here's the important point Luther makes about proper righteousness: "This righteousness is the product of the righteousness of the first type, actually its fruit and consequence."[10] Get the order here: first Christ's righteousness for us, then our own. Calvin puts it this way: "Unless you first of all grasp what your relationship to God is, and the nature of his judgment concerning you, you have neither a foundation on which to establish your salvation nor one on which to build piety toward God."[11]

A man tends to live up to his self-image. Forgiven or condemned, righteous or filthy—how we perceive ourselves makes all the difference in the world. For all of us, the adventure of a fruitful life begins only after we've settled once for all who we really are. Knowledge is power, and knowledge of our truest selves empowers us to face our weaknesses and failings head on—not as impotent victims, but as victors in Christ.

God's Story Meets Our Stories

In the previous chapter, I used the language of "story" to describe the various causes of apathy. The basic idea was that there is a backstory to the apathy that each of us experiences, and all our backstories differ one from another. The question I want to address in the remainder of this chapter is: How does the grand

9 Martin Luther, "Two Kinds of Righteousness," in *Martin Luther: Selections from His Writings*, ed. John Dillenberger (New York: Anchor, 1962), 86–87.

10 Luther, "Two Kinds of Righteousness," 88–89.

11 Calvin, *Institutes*, 3.11.1.

story of God's rescue connect with the little stories behind our apathy?

The triune God is the answer to every question, the solution to our deepest problems. That sounds nice, I'm sure, and few Christians would disagree with the general sentiment. However, how does the good news of Jesus Christ address the real-life causes of apathy? How is the good news the *ongoing* cure for apathy? Or are these just dumb questions, futile attempts to try and bring together two things that are really unrelated? I don't think so. I am convinced that God is the gospel; he's the great news, great reward, and great satisfier of all our needs.[12] If so, then what does he offer us in our doubt, grief, triviality, feelings of inadequacy, lack of discipline, fragility, and purposelessness? And how might God's way with us help in our fight against relentless apathy? Let's explore this a bit.

Doubt Meets Patience

Toward the end of Jude's letter, he counsels the church, "Have mercy on those who doubt" (Jude 22). In many ways, this is God's heart toward us, the doubting Thomases of the world.

We see this often in Scripture. For example, when the people of Israel seem to question and doubt God's love for them, he doesn't explode in a tirade. The book of Malachi begins with a conversation between the Lord and his doubting people:

> "I have loved you," says the LORD. But you say, "How have you loved us?" "Is not Esau Jacob's brother?" declares the LORD. "Yet I have loved Jacob but Esau I have hated. (Mal. 1:2–3)

12 I borrow the language of "God is the gospel" from John Piper, *God Is the Gospel: Meditations on God's Love as the Gift of Himself* (Wheaton, IL: Crossway, 2011).

Rather than crushing the people for their doubts, God bears with them, even answering their insulting question. He reaffirms his love for Israel and reminds the people of the concrete ways he's shown them favor.

One of my favorite Gospel stories is the account of Jesus's healing of the boy oppressed by a mute spirit. His disciples try to heal the boy but fail. The boy's father then comes to Jesus, saying, "If you can do anything, have compassion on us and help us." Jesus responds, "All things are possible for one who believes." Then comes the father's response that encapsulates so much of my Christian life: "I believe; help my unbelief" (Mark 9:22–24). To the man suspended between belief and unbelief—in other words, to all doubters—Jesus responds with patience and mercy. He gives him what he wants. He heals the man's son.

Jesus bears with us amid our doubt. He is even willing to accommodate us. On two occasions after his resurrection, Jesus's disciples doubt that he has done what he promised. In Luke 24, the risen Jesus appears to his huddled disciples. They are startled and frightened, thinking they are encountering a spirit. Jesus, knowing that they are filled with doubt that it is actually him in the flesh, directs them to his wounds. Yet, this isn't enough: "They still did not believe it because of joy and amazement" (Luke 24:41 NIV). So, Jesus takes a piece of fish and eats it before their very eyes. He proves to them that he is truly alive again.

He didn't have to do this. But his loving patience is shown in a concrete way: he does what he can to remove their doubts.

Jesus's treatment of Thomas, who clearly is not the only doubting disciple, also shows God's mercy and truth encountering our doubt. First, he kindly directs Thomas to touch his wounds and, as a result, "stop doubting and believe" (John 20:27 NIV). The very proofs that Thomas asks for (v. 25) are granted him by the Lord. Second, however, Jesus doesn't necessarily praise doubt. In fact, he says it's better to believe without getting visible proofs (v. 29). Nevertheless, he grants them on occasion. The gospel is the good news of a patient God, who bears with those who doubt his presence even as they look him squarely in the face.

Grief Meets Hope

Grief keeps us anchored to the past, fearful, and self-preserving. It often eats away at our desire to engage with our lives. To the grieving and disappointed, Jesus says, "Blessed are those who mourn, for they shall be comforted" (Matt. 5:4) and "Blessed are those who weep now, for you shall laugh" (Luke 6:21). God confronts our grief with hope.

Numerous psychological studies have found that those with hope do better in life. One study, for instance, saw a close relationship between hope and academic and athletic success: those with more hope did better in both departments.[13] Hope is commonly defined by psychologists as something like "the sum of your mental willpower and waypower that you have for your goals."[14] Hope is a goal we have the will and a pathway to accomplish. Is this what God offers us—a goal, a will, and a way? Sort of, but not really.

The psychologists are correct that hope is essential for a vibrant life. God gives us hope of his constant care in this life (Matt.

13 Lewis A. Curry et al., "Role of Hope in Academic and Sport Achievement," *Journal of Personality and Social Psychology* 73 (1997): 1257–67.
14 Cited from C. R. Snyder, *The Psychology of Hope: You Can Get Here from There* (New York: The Free Press, 1994), 5.

28:20), and Paul even expresses confidence in God delivering him from "deadly peril" (2 Cor. 1:10). Yet, the hope God offers in the storm of suffering is the hope of creation's healing and transformation. In fact, Paul says that, when we were saved, we were brought into this hope (Rom. 8:24). Peter says we were born again into a "living hope" through the resurrection of Jesus (1 Pet. 1:3). Ultimately, the hope we are offered is not just for this life; it's not just that things will get better soon. Paul says that Christians would be the most pitiful people if our hope were anchored solely to this life (1 Cor. 15:19). One of the key hopes Scripture seems to regularly hold out is the hope of our own transformation and glory (Rom. 5:2; Gal. 5:5; Col. 1:27). In other words, God promises that he is going to bring good out of sadness, futility, and suffering—the good of making us like Jesus (Rom. 8:28–30). So, Paul prays earnestly that we "may know what is the hope to which he has called [us]" (Eph. 1:18) and "that by the power of the Holy Spirit [we] may abound in hope" (Rom. 15:13).

How we process grief and disappointment is bound up with how connected we are with our Christian hope. We're told that we are not to "grieve like the rest of mankind, who have no hope" (1 Thess. 4:13 NIV). Why? Because we believe that Jesus Christ really rose from the dead and will raise everyone who belongs to him (v. 14). These truths are supposed to be uplifting and perspective-giving. We are even told to "encourage one another with these words" (v. 18).

The cynical may view all this as Pollyannaish, head-in-the-clouds thinking that does no practical good. Wishing upon a star doesn't accomplish much. True, but Christian hope is real and provides energy to move us forward. Paul writes, "Since we have such a hope"—the hope of real transformation, the hope of future glory—"we are very bold" (2 Cor. 3:12). Hope emboldens us to face the meaningful challenges of today. John writes that the hope that we will one day be like Christ is the motivation to strive to be like him: "Everyone who thus hopes in him purifies himself as he is pure" (1 John 3:3). Someone could easily think: If it's guaranteed that I'm eventually going to be like Christ, why bother now? John's statement is counterintuitive. Hope energizes. It doesn't deflate.

In his landmark "I Have a Dream" speech, Martin Luther King Jr. eloquently spells out the connection between hope and action:

> I have a dream that one day every valley shall be exalted, every hill and mountain shall be made low, the rough places will be made plain, and the crooked places will be made straight, and the glory of the Lord shall be revealed, and all flesh shall see it together.
>
> This is our hope. This is the faith that I go back to the South with. With this faith we will be able to hew out of the mountain of despair a stone of hope. With this faith we will be able to transform the jangling discords of our nation into a beautiful symphony of brotherhood. With this faith we will be able to work together, to pray together, to struggle together, to go to jail together, to stand up for freedom together, knowing that we will be free one day.[15]

The biblical imagery is obvious. But notice that Christian hope gave King and others the strength and drive to engage in the messy

---

15 Martin Luther King Jr., "I Have a Dream" Address, https://kinginstitute.stanford.edu/.

work of civil rights and racial justice in the 1960s. Hope has the power to release our grip on the past, finger by finger, so that we are freed to live fully in the present. This energizing, motivating, and enlivening hope is what God offers us in our grief.

Triviality Meets Perspective

We are drowning in triviality. It's no wonder we find ourselves losing perspective about what really matters and not caring about much at times. A soft nihilism—a fancy word for the feeling that everything is kind of meaningless—tends to creep in easily and undetected. Yet, amid this fog, God steps in.

My church has a line we repeat regularly as a sort of vision statement: "We want to offer people a better story and better family." This simple message highlights how inhabiting a story—in this case, God's story—can be transformative. One author writes, "We tell ourselves stories in order to live."[16] In other words, our stories provide perspective and help us make sense of the world. When we lack a large, life-unifying story, we find ourselves in the Wild West of small narratives (e.g., about money, fame, or power) that end up providing no meaning, no perspective, and only greater confusion about what is significant. Thankfully, however, God tells us who we are, our place in his drama, and what really matters.

It struck me recently how often the preachers in the book of Acts give a full recounting of the history of Israel and even the history of humanity in their sermons (see Acts 2, 3, 7, 13, and 17). It's as if they're saying to their audiences, "If you want to

16 Joan Didion, *The White Album* (New York: Farrar, Straus and Giroux, 1979), 11.

know the significance of these events, you need to know the story in which they are placed." Or maybe they're saying, "If you want to discern whether these are really meaningful events or merely flashes in the pan, we must narrate your history." These histories helped those early hearers of the gospel message discern what was truly meaningful and worthy of their attention, and they do the same for us.

When Jesus's disciples return from a short-term mission trip feeling good about their ability to cast out demons, Jesus redirects them. He points them to what really matters: "Do not rejoice in this, that the spirits are subject to you, but rejoice that your names are written in heaven" (Luke 10:20). Similarly, when the disciples are enamored by the beauty and grandeur of the temple, he refocuses them by telling them about the end of history (21:5–36). He remarks that not a single stone of that glorious temple will be left standing when all is said and done. In other words, in light of the bigger thing that God is doing, Jesus is saying that his followers shouldn't focus on power, wealth, or even beauty. These are not the major themes in God's drama. They are fleeting. The story of what God is doing is as old as creation: to reconcile all things to himself through Christ (Col. 1:20).

A passage that often takes my breath away is the closing statement in the final book of C. S. Lewis's Narnia series. Speaking of the heroes and heroines of his series, he writes,

And for us this is the end of all the stories, and we can most truly say that they all lived happily ever after. But for them it was only the beginning of the real story. All their life in this world and all their adventures in Narnia had only been the cover and the title page: now at last they were beginning Chapter One of the Great Story which no one on earth has read: which goes on forever: in which every chapter is better than the one before.[17]

What is true for those characters is true for us. Just as we misunderstand the adventures in Narnia if we don't view them as the cover and title page, so we can't understand the events of our day or their significance unless we place them in their ultimate context. God invites us into the bigger drama and provides us with meaning, proportion, and perspective. He calls us back to what is truly awesome.

Inadequacy Meets Significance

A few years ago, sociologist James Davison Hunter expressed skepticism regarding Christians' ability to actually change the world, especially in the ways we commonly talk about in our schools, mission agencies, and churches. He writes of the common mindset of Christians,

> At the end of the day, the message is clear: even if not in the lofty realms of political life that he was called to, you too can be a Wilberforce. In your own sphere of influence, you too can be an Edwards, a Dwight, a Booth, a Lincoln, a Churchill, a Dorothy Day, a Martin Luther King, a Mandela, a Mother Teresa, a Vaclav Havel, a John Paul II, and so on. If you have the courage and hold to the right values and if you think Christianly

---

17 C. S. Lewis, *The Last Battle* (New York: HarperTrophy, 1984), 228.

with an adequate Christian worldview, you too can change the world. *This account is almost wholly mistaken.*[18]

Hunter argues that political reform, social justice advocacy, and even evangelism, while they do produce some good, really do not change the world. In fact, he goes on to say that it is certainly not the average Christian, or even individuals per se, who changes the world. Elites who have access to power or are connected to powerful institutions are really the ones who change the world—for good or bad. Change flows from the top down, not from the bottom up.[19]

Hunter's book is provocative and well worth reading. But it is not difficult to see how his claims can lend (often depressing) support to our feelings of being inconsequential and insignificant. If I can't change the world, am I significant? Do I even matter?

To those who feel insignificant, and who in the culture's eyes are inconsequential, Jesus reveals the Father's heart. He tells us, "Are not five sparrows sold for two pennies? And not one of them is forgotten before God. Why, even the hairs of your head are all numbered. Fear not; you are of more value than many sparrows" (Luke 12:6–7). We all want to be seen, not looked past. Jesus reminds those who feel invisible that they have a Father who knows them deeply and intimately, and who cares for them. Later, he tells his followers, "Fear not, little flock, for it is your Father's good pleasure to give you the kingdom" (v. 32). We are each a part of

18 James Davison Hunter, *To Change the World: The Irony, Tragedy, and Possibility of Christianity in the Late Modern World* (New York: Oxford University Press, 2010), 16–17 (emphasis added).

19 See Hunter, *To Change the World*, chap. 4.

God's little flock and are greatly valued by him. He takes immense pleasure in giving us the honor of being citizens of his kingdom.

Not only are we not inconsequential in God's eyes, but the things we do are not worthless. God promises that whatever good we pursue in this life will be rewarded, and that in due season, we will reap a harvest if we don't give up (Gal. 6:9). God will not forget the big or small, well-known or hidden things we do as his faithful servants. Everything is valued, and everything will be rewarded.

God tells us that, in the final analysis, we are far from inconsequential. He confronts our "Why bother?" attitude with the good news that we matter to him. And whatever matters to God is of ultimate and eternal significance.

Lack of Discipline Meets an Easy Yoke

For those of us who, for one reason or another, lack discipline and consistency in the practices of our spiritual lives, drawing near to God may feel like an ever-increasing burden too heavy to bear. We may be aware that our apathy flows from our lack of regular engagement with the things of the Spirit, yet may feel helpless and hopeless to change anything. What does God have to say to people like us?

Interestingly enough, he tells us that he wants to put a yoke on us, yet he promises that his yoke will not be a heavy one. Jesus says, "Come to me, all who labor and are heavy laden, and I will give you rest. Take my yoke upon you, and learn from me, for I am gentle and lowly in heart, and you will find rest for your souls. For my yoke is easy, and my burden is light" (Matt. 11:28–30).

To those of us who feel burdened by the seemingly countless things we *could* do to draw close to God, Jesus promises a lighter burden and true rest. He doesn't pretend that the work God wants to do in us will be free of any yoke. Yet, he promises to not overburden us and that his yoke—whatever it is—will result in what we most desire: Sabbath rest for our souls.

Why is his yoke lighter? One Bible scholar responds, "They will find Jesus' yoke light because he is a Master who will care for them (Mt 11:29). Jesus' yoke is not lighter because he demands less, but because he bears more of the load with us."[20] Unlike the religious leaders of his day (and ours), Jesus does what it takes to bring us rest, now and eternally. He is with us as our helper. He helps carry what seems to be a real burden, if we will receive his offer.

You see, the gospel is not just the good news of what God has done for us and will do for us in the future; it is also the great news of his presence with us right now. In a passage I mentioned briefly in the last chapter, the apostle Paul connects God's presence to his difficult spiritual labors: "[God's] grace toward me was not in vain. On the contrary, I worked harder than any of them, though it was not I, but the grace of God that is with me" (1 Cor. 15:10). Grace does not refer here merely to God's love for Paul. Rather, it's best to see grace as divine power that flows from God's love. Grace is power. Grace does work. In this case, grace is the presence and power of God in Paul's life that enables him to work hard for the cause of the gospel. Elsewhere, Paul writes that the grace of God trains us "to renounce ungodliness and worldly passions, and to live self-controlled, upright, and godly lives in the present age" (Titus 2:12).

---

20 Craig S. Keener, *Matthew* (Downers Grove, IL: InterVarsity Press, 1997), 222.

In other words, God's grace teaches our hearts discipline; it trains our desires, inspires self-control, and moves us to live sober and countercultural lives. In both passages, Paul is stating what Jesus implies. God is with us and in us to help us carry the yoke he's given us. The gospel of God's grace is the promise of his very real help even as we stumble our way toward discipline and diligence.

Fragility Meets Peace

Over the last decade or so, a movement has arisen among parents who are concerned that we are overprotecting our kids and inhibiting their growth into adulthood. "Free-range parenting"—the name of the philosophy of parenting adopted by this group—was made popular by journalist Lenore Skenazy, who caught the public's attention when she chronicled how she allowed her nine-year-old son to take the New York City subway home on his own. Skenazy's website has a mission statement of sorts that represents this movement well: "Fighting the belief that our children are in constant danger from creeps, kidnapping, germs, grades, flashers, frustration, failure, baby snatchers, bugs, bullies, men, sleepovers and/or the perils of a non-organic grape." The philosophy is simple: when we unnecessarily shield children from perceived risk, we stunt their independence and maturity.[21]

Regardless of what we may think about Skenazy's parenting, there is a sense in which Christ has called us to "free-range" discipleship. We are invited into a life of risk-taking, but it's risk-taking with a promise. Jesus says, "For whoever would save his

---

21 Free-Range Kids website, https://www.freerangekids.com/.

life will lose it, but whoever loses his life for my sake will find it" (Matt. 16:25). There is a principle buried beneath this beautiful promise. Those who want to be self-protecting and self-preserving will find themselves feeling more and more dead inside. Abundant life comes from stepping into the fray rather than stepping out of it. Those who put themselves in the path of potential pain, especially pain that comes from caring about the things God cares about, will receive one hundred times what the self-protective fear they'll lose (Mark 10:29–30). A lost life is not a wasted life.[22]

But even beneath these wonderful promises lies another precious promise, one that has stuck with me since my first days as a Christian. After telling his disciples that hardships are a natural and expected part of the Christian life, Jesus comforts them with the assurance that he has "overcome the world" (John 16:33). Jesus declares his victory over the world and all it can do to him. To disciples who he knows will desert him in due course, he announces that through his apparent defeat on the cross, he has conquered the powers of this world. He encourages his weak disciples that they should have peace because those who are in him share in his victory. Our past, present, and future enemies have already been defeated. The future need not be threatening.[23]

This is the salvation offered in the gospel, and it dispels the fear that would keep us disengaged from potentially difficult things. Antifragility does not come from merely putting ourselves in hard situations. It comes primarily from receiving Christ's promises and resting in them.

22 John Piper, *Don't Waste Your Life* (Wheaton, IL: Crossway, 2003), 79–80.
23 Edward W. Klink III, *John*, Zondervan Exegetical Commentary on the New Testament 4 (Grand Rapids, MI: Zondervan, 2016), 701–4.

Purposelessness Meets a Reason for Being

I've never been a huge fan of church or business purpose statements. They often seem contrived or too copycat. After a while, they all start to blur together and lose their punch.

Of course, this isn't always the case. I can still remember a few purpose statements, even after twenty or more years. For instance, one popular ministry has the purpose statement "We exist to spread a passion for the supremacy of God in all things . . ." There's also my former campus ministry's statement: "We are here to change the world by helping turn lost students into Christ-centered laborers." These purpose statements have stuck with me because God used them to energize me and move me to action. We all need a sense of purpose large enough and worthy enough to inspire us.

Theologian Thaddeus Williams speaks of the importance of worshiping something with enough *kavod*, the Hebrew term for glory or weightiness. He insists on three marks of *kavod*. First, that which we worship must be a "first thing," that is, a supremely important thing, not some secondary good. Second, it must be unbreakable, not brittle, and therefore able to bear the weight of our devotion. Finally, it must be like the sun, not a spotlight, and able to shed light on every dimension of our lives.[24] In short, the only thing worthy of worship and devotion, worthy of orienting our lives around, is God himself.

That is exactly what Christ offers us as a life purpose. Jesus prays, "Father, the hour has come; glorify your Son that the Son may glorify you, since you have given him authority over all flesh,

---

24 Thaddeus J. Williams, *Reflect: Becoming Yourself by Mirroring the Greatest Person in History* (Wooster: Weaver, 2017), 8–13.

to give eternal life to all whom you have given him. And this is eternal life, that they know you, the only true God, and Jesus Christ whom you have sent" (John 17:1–3).

Christ's purpose is to bring glory to the Father by giving eternal life to his followers. But notice how he describes eternal life: it is knowing the Father and Son. What God wants most for us and from us is that we know him. That is real life. That is our reason for being. It is the one thing that should wake us up from our apathetic slumber. We are made to know him. Thus, everything we do is to serve the purpose of knowing God.

In a very real sense, Christ died to purchase purpose for us. He redeems us from aimless and meandering ways of living, not only by forgiving our shortcomings, but by giving us a new re-orienting focus. He says, "Follow me, and I will make you fishers of men" (Matt. 4:19)—salvation and purpose go hand in hand. Jesus says we can get up every morning with a purpose so grand and so rich that it will never be incapable of scratching our itch for the meaningful.

The All-Important Eucatastrophe

A popular rapper recently released a song with this lyric: "Use this gospel for protection, it's a hard road to heaven."[25] Though I liked the song, the line struck me as odd. "Use" the gospel? It seemed to be (mis)treating the gospel like a kind of inoculation. But as I thought about it some more, I realized there was more than an ounce of truth there. What God has done for us, the good news, is our protection against lies about ourselves, about the possibility

25 Kanye West, "Use This Gospel," on *Jesus Is King*, Getting Out Our Dreams II/Def Jam Recordings/Anthem Entertainment, 2019.

of change, and about God's opinion of us. All these lies cripple us in our fight against apathy. In fact, what I've been arguing in this chapter is that we need to "use" this gospel before we (and as we) try to thaw ourselves out of our apathy.

No matter what path we may have taken to arrive at Apathyville, God wants to redirect us toward the path of life. He does this by offering patience, hope, perspective, significance, an easy yoke, peace, and purpose. He also tells us we are forgiven, free, and healed (in the past), and that he is forgiving, freeing, and healing us (in the present). This is the air we breathe as Christians—the air of grace and possibility, of God's love and a living hope. The good news of God continues to offer apathetic people everything we need for godliness.

J. R. R. Tolkien coined a term to describe the unexpected happy turn in a fairy tale that floods our hearts with joy. He called it *eucatastrophe* (or "good catastrophe") and describes it as a "sudden and miraculous grace." He goes on to say,

> [Eucatastrophe] does not deny the existence of *dyscatastrophe*, of sorrow and failure: the possibility of these is necessary to the joy of deliverance; it denies (in the face of much evidence, if you will) universal final defeat and in so far is *evangelium* [gospel], giving a fleeting glimpse of Joy, Joy beyond the walls of the world, poignant as grief. It is the mark of a good fairy-story.[26]

For Tolkien, the gospel, the story that is not merely a story, is the greatest of all fairy tales and the resurrection the greatest of all

26 J. R. R. Tolkien, *The Tolkien Reader* (New York: Ballantine, 1966), 86.

eucatastrophes. "The Birth of Christ is the eucatastrophe of Man's history. The Resurrection is the eucatastrophe of the story of the Incarnation. This story begins and ends in joy. . . . There is no tale ever told that men would rather find was true, and none which so many sceptical men have accepted as true on its own merits."[27]

Our weaknesses and sins seem tragic and catastrophic. Yet, we often approach them as if the eucatastrophic moment hasn't happened yet. May we allow the greatest story to swallow up our stories, to reframe them, to put them in their biggest and most important context. May we find joy in the happy ending of the gospel. May we come to know that we the apathetic are defined by the love that will not let us go, the light that illumines the dark places of our souls, the joy that seeks us, and the cross (and resurrection) that lifts us from despair. This is when the battle against apathy truly becomes a struggle rather than merely a surrender.

Questions for Reflection

1. What aspect of the good news was particularly encouraging to you?

2. In light of the gospel, how specifically might God be calling you to respond to your apathy?

3. Can you think of other ways the gospel might intersect with apathy that were not addressed in this chapter?

---

27 Tolkien, *Tolkien Reader*, 88–89.

5

Wax On, Wax Off

Ways to Combat Apathy

ONE OF THE INDISPUTABLY best films of the 1980s was about a high school misfit who had recently moved to California to start a new life with his single mom. Kind of scrawny, and not quite the California surfer type, Daniel LaRusso is picked on regularly by a gang of cool kids who happen to be karate students at Cobra Kai, a local dojo. On one fateful night, he is brutally beaten up by this group, only to be rescued by the handyman of his apartment complex, Mr. Miyagi. Daniel learns that the unassuming repairman is a karate master. Without hesitation, he asks Miyagi to train him in martial arts, but the handyman declines. Yet, after witnessing on a different occasion the cruelty and unreasonableness of these students and their *sensei*, Miyagi changes his mind and agrees to train Daniel for an upcoming tournament against the students of Cobra Kai.

Daniel's training sessions start off with a whimper. Rather than learning roundhouse kicks and death blows, he's given mundane tasks such as sanding floors, painting fences, and waxing Miyagi's cars. Frustrated, Daniel blows up at his teacher, complaining that he's learned nothing and that he's being used to do Miyagi's grunt work. Then comes one of the best scenes, where Miyagi helps Daniel see the meaning of the menial tasks. The painting motion, the repetitive movements involved in sanding a floor, and the circles Daniel makes when waxing the car are all key defensive moves in karate. "Wax on, wax off"—put the wax on the car, wipe the wax off the car—he's told repeatedly as he makes little circles with his hands. Daniel has to learn the hard lesson that karate skills don't get beamed down from outer space. He has to train himself to be a fighter by doing seemingly unhelpful things—things that feel disconnected from karate and, thus, appear to be a big waste of time. He needs to see that the skills and instincts required to excel in karate come only through repetitive practices—in his case, those performed during manual labor.

Practice forms habits, which in turn form us. The things we do repeatedly become near-automatic behaviors, and these behaviors shape our hearts. How does one become a kind person? By regularly practicing kindness. How does someone become a giving person? By making a practice of giving regularly. We become what we do.

Combat through Cultivation

As we consider preventing and overcoming apathy, it's best to think in terms of a long-term strategy rather than a short-term fix. Dallas Willard, speaking of the vital need for a long-term mentality, writes,

Those who say we cannot truly follow Christ turn out to be correct in a sense. We cannot behave "on the spot" as he did and taught if in the rest of our time we live as everybody else does. The "on the spot" episodes are not the place where we can, even by the grace of God, redirect unchristlike but ingrained tendencies of action toward sudden Christlikeness. Our efforts to take control *at that moment* will fail so uniformly and ingloriously that the whole project of following Christ will appear ridiculous to the watching world.[1]

I don't believe we handle apathy by trying something "on the spot" or attempting something once. The best way to deal with apathy is by developing a new way of living, thinking, and feeling. We fight it by being formed in particular directions, by incrementally becoming new people. We combat it by cultivating virtues and different attitudes.

On top of this, I think the best mode of attack is an indirect one. We combat apathy not by simply telling ourselves to stop being apathetic, but by addressing its various interconnected causes. Think of it as cutting off the enemy's food and water supply or stealing his ammunition. We defeat apathy by cultivating thoughts, feelings, and attitudes that counteract the sources of our indifference—grief, doubt, triviality, and so on. And, again, we cultivate these ways of living by practice. All of this may simply be a way of understanding Paul's exhortations to "put on Christ" (Gal. 3:27; see also Rom. 13:14). It seems that Paul is calling us to play dress-up, or as C. S. Lewis puts it, to pretend until the

1   Dallas Willard, *The Spirit of the Disciplines: Understanding How God Changes Lives* (New York: HarperCollins, 1991), 7.

pretense becomes a reality.[2] To "put on Christ" may be another way of saying "act like Christ so that you may truly become like Christ."

This chapter is an invitation to put on Christ. Along the way, I suggest practices that can enable us to do so in specific ways, namely, by cultivating honesty, affection, meaning, generosity, and fortitude. I hope that these daily, weekly, monthly, and yearly practices will become habits that help form in us apathy-fighting attitudes and postures of the soul. While I suggest a number of helps, no one should expect to do all or even many of these practices. That would be overwhelming. But I hope you will find one or two to put into practice and see how God meets you through them.

A Word on the Gospel, the Spirit, and Virtues

One more thing should be said before we dive into these practices. All talk about practices, habits, and virtues is sub-Christian if it does not have at the forefront Christ's work as well as the power of the Holy Spirit.

In the last chapter, we focused on the promise of healing, forgiveness, and freedom we receive through Christ. Yet, I waited till this point to mention one other crucial feature of the gospel's good news. The apostle Paul writes, "Christ redeemed us from the curse of the law by becoming a curse for us . . . so that we might receive the promised Spirit through faith" (Gal. 3:13–14). In other words, one of the things being announced in the gospel is the wonderful gift of the Holy Spirit. The Spirit is the "river of living

---

2   C. S. Lewis, *Mere Christianity* (Glasgow: Collins, 1977), 158–59.

water" (John 7:38), our source of life. According to Augustine, he is the greatest gift of God since he is the one who inspires love of God and neighbor in us. "Nothing is more excellent than this gift," he writes.[3]

Why does this matter for our discussion? God has given us a gift greater than any master teacher such as Miyagi could ever give. He has given us one who not only instructs us, but also empowers us and transforms us as we cooperate with him. Whatever we are going to say about practices and habits must be said with the ready acknowledgment that it is the Spirit who gives the desire, enables us to act on it, and bears fruit from our actions. The Spirit alone can turn a cold, stony, apathetic heart into a heart of flesh. Only the Spirit can make us lovers of God. And the Spirit does this as we seek to concretely apply the truths of God's word to our everyday lives.

With that said, let's begin our journey of cultivation.

Cultivate Honesty (in Community)

Apathy is a sickness from which we need healing. As with other illnesses, brutal honesty about our symptoms is critical for our recovery. Imagine sitting with a doctor and lying about your symptoms, or simply remaining silent. How can the doctor help you? Or, imagine the doctor keeping the truth of your illness from you. How can you move toward healing if you don't know what's really wrong? Honesty is essential if you're ever going to get better.

Honesty for the Christian must take the form of confession, not just before God but also before other believers. "Confess your

---

3 Augustine, *The Trinity*, ed. John E. Rotelle, trans. Edmund Hill (Hyde Park, NY: New City, 2012), 15.5, 424.

sins to one another and pray for one another, that you may be healed" (James 5:16). Christians are pushed out of the relative safety of private confession to the risky act of public honesty. But God's agenda is not to humiliate us; he's zealous for our healing, and has given us others to help facilitate it.

Dietrich Bonhoeffer reflected a great deal on the importance of confession in community and the dangers of doing life in isolation. He writes, "Those who remain alone with their evil are left utterly alone." In other words, there is no greater loneliness than when Christians are unable to confess their sins to one another. Even when we might be busy together, doing Bible studies or serving in ministry, we are truly alone if we cannot share our faults. This matters because, as Bonhoeffer goes on to say, "the more lonely people become, the more destructive the power of sin over them." He adds, "Sin wants to remain unknown, . . . [but] sin that has been spoken and confessed has lost all of its power."[4] Other believers have the role of extending and pronouncing God's forgiveness and healing. Yet, this doesn't happen, it *can't* happen, until we bring our sins out in the open.

It may feel very counterintuitive to some of us, but it is a deeply biblical truth that God gives a measure of authority to the church to "loose and bind" and to restore or not restore (Matt. 18:15–20; 1 Cor. 5:1–13). This function is not inconsequential or merely symbolic; it has ramifications for people's spiritual lives and vitality. Bonhoeffer speaks of the "breakthroughs" Christians can experience when we confess our sins to one another. Two of these breakthroughs are especially relevant. First, we experience a

4   Dietrich Bonhoeffer, *Life Together and Prayerbook of the Bible*, ed. Geffrey B. Kelly, trans. Daniel W. Bloesch and James H. Burtness (Minneapolis: Fortress, 1996), 108–10.

breakthrough *to the cross*. "By confessing actual sins the old self dies a painful, humiliating death before the eyes of another Christian." When we confess, we experience the cross as a form of humiliation *and* as the way to deliverance. Death must come before life. And this leads to a second breakthrough—the breakthrough *to new life*. Only through the cross do we experience resurrection power. In confession, we die to our old life, renounce our sin, and receive the power to walk in newness of life.[5]

Owning our wrongs also produces a resolve to become better people. One study showed how recalling our past immoral behaviors helps prepare us to pursue righteous behavior.[6] Another study found that those who only partially confess their faults feel worse than those who fully confess or don't confess at all.[7] If in our honesty we find ourselves concealing things out of a concern for self-protection, we only end up hurting ourselves. The road to renewal begins with honesty, with confession.

Very few stories capture this as powerfully as Fyodor Dostoyevsky's *Crime and Punishment*. The main character, Raskolnikov, has committed a double homicide and, after a long while, decides to confess the murder to compassionate and loving Sonia. She does not reject him, but amid her horror feels sympathy for him. At first, he offers only a partial confession riddled with self-justification, but eventually he makes a full confession to the authorities. Raskolnikov is sentenced to eight years of penal

---

5   Bonhoeffer, *Life Together*, 111–13.

6   Jennifer Jordan, Elizabeth Mullen, and J. Murnighan, "Striving for the Moral Self: The Effects of Recalling Past Moral Actions on Future Moral Behavior," *Personality & Social Psychology Bulletin* 37 (2011): 701–13.

7   E. Peer, A. Acquisti, and S. Shalvi, "I Cheated, but Only a Little": Partial Confessions to Unethical Behavior," *Journal of Personality and Social Psychology* 106 (2014): 202–17.

servitude. After some time in prison, his heart begins to soften. He remembers Sonia's kindness and mercy. He begins to see the possibility of becoming a new man. His story ends as a new beginning, what Dostoyevsky calls "the story of the gradual renewal of a man, the story of his gradual regeneration, of his passing from one world into another, of his initiation into a new unknown life."[8] Out of the death to self that comes through confession springs new life.

Many of us are in need of a breakthrough regarding apathy. Scripture invites us to experience the healing power of honesty. Confession to others helps remove the burden of our sin sickness. It also empowers others to help us avoid sin through prayer, their positive example, and practical interventions. Apathy, like other sicknesses, thrives when dwelling in the dark alone. According to one sixth-century writer, it "is a constant companion of the hermit."[9] In honest confession, we are dragging our apathy into the light. Honesty is not about being self-hating and self-deprecating; it's about embracing the truth of our situation. Honesty is about owning our true selves—including sins—before God and other people so that we can experience healing.

All this points to the necessity of living in community with other Christians. Being part of the church is "part of the fabric of redemption."[10] God is the only one who has no need of community outside of himself. Our disconnection from community

---

8 Fyodor Dostoyevsky, *Crime and Punishment*, trans. Constance Garnett, Great Classic Library (London: Chancellor, 1994), 455.

9 John Climacus, *The Ladder of Divine Ascent*, trans. Lazarus Moore (New York: Harper & Brothers), 52, http://www.prudencetrue.com/.

10 Eugene H. Peterson, *A Long Obedience in the Same Direction: Discipleship in an Instant Society* (Downers Grove, IL: InterVarsity Press, 1980), 169.

is an implicit pretense of deity, a claim to a sort of divine self-sufficiency. While it is true that only Christ breaks the power of canceled sin, the words and actions of fellow Christians announce to us that we are accepted (and called higher). The community helps break the power of recurring sin. As one writer puts it, "Divine acceptance is communicated to us through people . . . Our image of ourselves is also based in part on whether our fellowmen accept us or reject us."[11] Community, confession, and healing go hand in hand.

Every virtue or posture I recommend in this chapter is directed at one or more causes of apathy. However, this first one has no single target. Honesty is a metavirtue, an entryway to other virtues and a weapon against all sources of apathy. How do we cultivate it?

Practices for Cultivating Honesty

1. *Find or initiate a spiritual community within your church.* Small groups, men's or women's Bible studies, Sunday school classes, and ministry teams can all be communities of openness, honesty, encouragement, and admonition, if we allow them to be. We're each responsible to foster that openness where appropriate. When a group isn't available, find someone else within the church with whom you can have regular times of meaningful fellowship. Why within the church? Because the church is God's instrument for discipline, correction, and restoration—what I call "accountability with teeth." Fellowship, as Dallas Willard put it, is what makes confession bearable—and, I would add, productive.[12]

---

11 Anthony A. Hoekema, *A Christian Looks at Himself* (Grand Rapids, MI: Eerdmans, 1975), 102.
12 Willard, *The Spirit of the Disciplines*, 188.

2. *Confess concretely.* When you pray, make it a habit to confess specific sins, not just general sinfulness. Similarly, when you confess to other people, name the specific sins. In the case of apathy, confess your indifference to God, but also confess how you are guilty of immersing yourself in the trivial; confess your doubts, your lack of hope, your lack of discipline—in other words, confess your sinful disposition *and* the things that contribute to it, such as bad habits. Generic confession is usually not really confession. I have to bring my specific contributions to my malaise into the light in order to experience forgiveness and healing. And in enduring the pain of confessing to another, I am experiencing the discomfort I should be feeling before a holy God. But I am also experiencing, through the other person, the mercy of a loving God.

3. *Choose to spend time with passionate people.* We know that "iron sharpens iron" (Prov. 27:17). We also know that those who walk with the "I don't care" folks will not bear fruit. We are profoundly shaped by the company we keep. "Whoever walks with the wise becomes wise" (13:20). Make a plan to spend regular time with people that care about stuff—people who model zeal for the right things—even if they're not your closest friends. Not only do we need to know we are forgiven and accepted, we also need to be called higher. Zealous people reflect back to us where we fall short as well as a possible future, and both are necessary for our growth.

Cultivate Affection

A chapter that seeks to offer possible remedies for apathy must address the wellspring of all our action and inaction—the heart. As I said earlier, the heart is the heart of the matter. We're apathetic because our hearts are alive to things that don't matter and numb to things that do. Our loves are disordered. As C. S. Lewis famously put it, we are far too easily pleased by lesser things.[13] We need a reawakening of love for the right things. We need to cultivate affection.

Stop It! Start It!

In a now classic *MAD TV* sketch, a patient, Catherine, visits a therapist, Dr. Switzer, played by Bob Newhart. Their conversation begins with Dr. Switzer explaining his billing policy—he charges $5 for the first five minutes, but nothing thereafter. Why? Because the session won't take much longer than five minutes. He then invites Catherine to share her issue. She discloses her fear of being buried alive in a box and how this fear is triggered any time she's in an enclosed environment. The following conversation ensues:

Switzer: Alright, well, let's go Catherine. I'm going to say two words to you right now. I want you to listen to them very, very carefully, then I want you to take them out of the office with you and incorporate them into your life.

Catherine: Shall I write them down?

Switzer: If it makes you comfortable. It's just two words. We find most people can remember them.

Catherine: Okay.

Switzer: You ready?

Catherine: Yes.

Switzer: Okay, here they are: STOP IT!

13 C. S. Lewis, "The Weight of Glory," in *The Weight of Glory and Other Addresses* (New York: HarperCollins, 2001), 26.

Catherine (puzzled): I'm sorry?

Switzer: STOP IT!

Catherine: Stop it?

Switzer: Yes. S-T-O-P, new word, I-T![14]

One reason this scene is hilarious is because we know that, on the one hand, it is not that easy to change our behaviors, emotions, or character. If change could come by simply telling ourselves to stop this or that, many of us would be incredible people. Yet, on the other hand, we sense that people can often overcomplicate what's needed to make a change. Sometimes we just want to tell friends and family members who are tangled up in various issues to just stop it.

In fact, we get this sense sometimes when we read the New Testament. For instance, the apostle Paul, without any further ado, simply tells us things like "Put away anger and slander" and "Put on compassionate hearts and humility" (see Col. 3:8–12). In fact, Paul simply exhorts us to rejoice with those who rejoice and weep with those who weep (Rom. 12:15). It's as if he's basically saying, "Stop this!" and "Start that!"

Some people may feel that it's unhelpful to tell an apathetic person to stop feeling apathy and start feeling zeal and passion. A person can't just turn these things off and on, we might think. However, it's equally unhelpful to believe that affections or attitudes cannot be developed or changed. In fact, the cultivating of affections such as love (not the instantaneous appearance of them) is a long-term strategy for battling apathy.

14 *Mad TV*, season 6, episode 24, directed by Bruce Leddy, May 12, 2001.

Being Affected

Let's return to our earlier definition of passion as the capacity "to be affected" by something. A prescription for healing apathy is a recovery of the ability to be affected. One author writes, "When we are not profoundly affected by the treasure in our grasp, apathy and mediocrity are inevitable."[15] What does he mean? The kingdom parable of Matthew 13:44 provides a perfect illustration: "The kingdom of heaven is like treasure hidden in a field, which a man found and covered up. Then in his joy he goes and sells all that he has and buys that field." The author creatively fleshes out the story, describing the actions of the man in the parable:

> He is deeply affected by his splendid find. A single thought absorbs him; in fact, it so controls him that he can no longer work undistracted by day or sleep undisturbed by night. The field must become his property!
>
> As a day laborer, it is impossible for him to take possession of the buried treasure. Where can he get the money to buy the field? Caution and discretion fly out the window. He sells everything he owns. He gets a fair price for his hut and the few sheep he has acquired. He turns to relatives, friends, and acquaintances and borrows significant sums. The owner of the field is delighted with the fancy price offered by the purchaser and sells to the peasant without a second thought.
>
> The new owner's wife is apoplectic [i.e., beside herself]. His sons are inconsolable. His friends reproach him. His neighbors

15   Brennan Manning, *Abba's Child: The Cry of the Heart for Intimate Belonging* (Colorado Springs: NavPress, 1994), 120.

wag their heads. . . . The peasant remains unruffled, even joyful, in the face of widespread opposition.[16]

Why is this man able to withstand criticism from loved ones and prudent advisors? How is he able to move forward when countless barriers stand in his way? It's simple: he has been gripped by the value of what is truly valuable. He knows deep down that he has stumbled upon riches beyond belief, and he's willing to do anything to lay hold of them.

Now, this parable is pointing to Jesus and his kingdom as the ultimate treasure. But we have to ask ourselves: In teaching this parable, is Jesus describing a one-time state of being that happens only at our conversion or is he saying that this should be the ongoing posture of all who are in the kingdom? Is this joy and affection something to which Jesus continually invites his followers, or is he saying that if we don't have it already, it's too late? I believe he's calling all of us to be constantly affected by the treasure of the kingdom. I believe he wants to open the eyes of our hearts so that we can truly feel, in our guts, his great worth.

The parable illustrates what the old preacher Thomas Chalmers called "the expulsive power of a new affection."[17] Just as the power of the peasant's joy (the new affection) overtakes his love for his property, so our affection for Christ can expel our affection for trivial things. One love replaces another. We defeat our selective apathy by cultivating stronger affections. We fight by replacement.

16 Manning, *Abba's Child*, 118.
17 Thomas Chalmers, *The Expulsive Power of New Affection* (Wheaton, IL: Crossway, 2020).

This is what Paul commands: he says we are to put off and put on; replace old attitudes with new ones. This is a real possibility, and it's a real necessity.

Perhaps it would help if we asked ourselves this question: *How do I grow in affection for my spouse, children, or friends?* This points us in the right direction because, as we wrestle with apathy, we are fundamentally wrestling with numbness toward a person, and not just toward Christian ideas or practices (though those are often equally mistreated).

So, how do we grow in affection?

Practices for Cultivating Affection

1. *Refuse to remove yourself from the presence of God (and the things he cherishs).* While it is sometimes true that absence makes the heart grow fonder, it is equally true that absence can breed disinterest and neglect. The less time I spend with my wife, the less connected I am with her heart—the things she's concerned or excited about. We've often heard of couples "growing apart" or "falling out of love" with each other. This is often a result of basic relationship neglect. I think this is all the more the case when the other person is God. Absence breeds vague feelings of guilt, but rarely makes the heart grow fonder. Also, as in other relationships, absence tempts us to believe lies about the other person, or about their love, faithfulness, and so on. So, we must resolve to not allow a day to go by without deliberately putting ourselves in the presence of the Lord. Refuse absence.

2. *Receive regular reminders of God's love for you.* Few things warm my heart like the birthday, Father's Day, anniversary, and

Christmas cards I receive from my wife every year. As a family and as a couple, we always aim to say meaningful and affirming things in the cards we write, and I love that. When my wife reminds me that she loves me, that she's in my corner, and that she's proud of me, I feel a small kindling of love in my own heart for her. We all like to be liked, and we tend to be more interested in people who show an interest in us. Brennan Manning writes, "The recovery of passion begins with the recovery of my true self as the beloved."[18] What will we sing, watch, listen to, read, talk about, and celebrate that will remind us that we are God's beloved? We have to build these reminders into our daily lives, beginning with meditating on God's word.

3. *Reflect on how your daily rituals are shaping your affections.* All day long, we are being encouraged to devote ourselves to a variety of things. This encouragement doesn't necessarily come in the form of words. James K. A. Smith speaks of our daily routines as "liturgies" that form us in profound ways. Affections such as love, or nonaffections such as apathy, are often more caught than taught. He thus calls us to "take a liturgical audit" of our lives. Practically speaking, this might involve taking time weekly or monthly to reflect on the rituals of our lives. Ask yourself: When I ritually go to Starbucks or the mall; fixate on my smartphone; fall asleep every night to a Netflix show; or weekly go to Disneyland, what am I being trained to desire? Ask what these routines are directing you to love or value as the good life.[19] Is it leisure? Is it pleasure? Is it ease? Is it recognition?

18 Manning, *Abba's Child*, 125.
19 See James K. A. Smith, *You Are What You Love: The Spiritual Power of Habit* (Grand Rapids, MI: Brazos, 2016), 53–55.

These are critical questions because you cannot love God and love _____ (fill in the blank).

4. *Reclaim fasting as a way of maintaining or reigniting your spiritual intensity.* Fasting (accompanied by prayer) is a way of awakening and preserving what John Piper calls "the hunger of homesickness for God." It is a way to wean us from good things that can become God-substitutes—such as TV, social media, leisure, and even food. Piper explains, "When I say that the root of Christian fasting is the hunger of homesickness for God, I mean that we will do anything and go without anything if, by any means, we might protect ourselves from the deadening effects of innocent delights and preserve the sweet longings of our homesickness for God."[20] Those of us already in the throes of apathy need to awaken longing; those who want to keep apathy at arm's length need to preserve longings for God. Fasting is a neglected aid on the road to passion. When we fast, we tell God, "This much, O God, I want you!"[21] Imagine how our appetites and affections could be formed if we made it a monthly practice to say this to the Lord through fasting!

Cultivate Meaning and Mission

Lurking under the surface of much of our apathy is a loss of a sense of meaning, purpose, and mission. We become foggy about what really matters and what we're really to be about. Doubt gives birth to a world without meaning, and being bombarded by the trivial also feeds into the meaninglessness of things. Os Guinness once

---

20 John Piper, *A Hunger for God: Desiring God through Fasting and Prayer* (Wheaton, IL: Crossway, 1997), 15.
21 Piper, *Hunger for God*, 23.

said, "As modern people, we have too much to live with and so little to live for."[22] We have time and money, but no meaning. We need to recapture our reason for being, a sense of our place and purpose in this world, as this gives meaning to all of our actions.

One Pure and Holy Passion

When I was in my early twenties, I loved a song that included a powerful cry for "one pure and holy passion" and "one glorious ambition": to know and follow Christ.[23] This song was powerful because it expressed a deep desire in me for God to take my many scattered interests and aspirations and unite them under one banner and purpose. The song was a prayer for God to cut through the confusion and focus my life on one thing, the most meaningful thing: him.

If you find yourself apathetic, God may be inviting you to revive your sense of purpose. If you've never had a sense of purpose, now is the time to gain one.

During the Second World War, C. S. Lewis preached a sermon at Oxford called "None Other Gods: Culture in War-Time" (later published as "Learning in War-Time"). The basic question he poses in the sermon is: What's the point of academic studies during a time of war? University studies would seem to be an extravagance at a time when life and civilization hang in the balance. Why not focus on things that have obvious eternal value, such as saving souls? He first responds by questioning the

---

22 Os Guinness, *The Call: Finding and Fulfilling the Central Purpose of Your Life* (Nashville: W Publishing, 2003), 4.

23 "One Pure and Holy Passion," words and music by Mark Altrogge, © 1988 Curb Dayspring Music, LLC | Sovereign Grace Praise.

value of *any* academic study, not merely in times of war, but also in times of peace, particularly in light of eternity, hell, and heaven. Every Christian student, he writes, "must ask himself how it is right, or even psychologically possible, for creatures who are every moment advancing either to heaven or to hell, to spend any fraction of the little time allowed them in this world on such comparative trivialities as literature or art, mathematics or biology."[24] Is it ever justifiable to indulge in these cultural activities? Are they not all mere trifles when eternity is always at stake?

Lewis is asking whether there is any meaning or purpose to the mission of the university. His response takes him to Paul's familiar exhortation in 1 Corinthians 10:31: "Whether you eat or drink, or whatever you do, do all to the glory of God." All human activities—even mundane ones like eating meals with friends—are infused with ultimate meaning when directed toward honoring God. Paul's words are our perpetual marching orders: glorify God in everything! That is the mission that provides meaning to everything we do. Lewis writes, "Before I became a Christian I do not think I fully realized that one's life, after conversion, would inevitably consist in doing most of the same things one had been doing before: one hopes, in a new spirit, but still the same things."[25] The "new spirit" is what Paul is talking about. He's instructing us to continue to do our academic work (for example), but not in the way we would have done it in the past. We are to do it in the new spirit of having God's glory—which

24 C. S. Lewis, "Learning in War-Time," in *Fern-seed and Elephants and Other Essays on Christianity*, ed. Walter Hooper (Glasgow: Fount, 1986), 27.

25 Lewis, "Learning in War-Time," 29.

often amounts to doing what is honoring to God and helpful to humanity—as our main aim and mission in life. Whether in wartime or peacetime, and even with eternity pressing in on us, what seem like trivialities can have ultimate significance if done in the "new spirit." And those trifles that cannot be done this way can be cast aside. You see, our sense of meaning and mission gives clarity to our day-to-day entanglements.

Many of us have lost that sense of meaning in our lives. We feel like we're floating from one event to another, one responsibility to the next, one task after another, but nothing feels cohesive. Everything feels scattered. There isn't one pure and holy passion to help stitch together the elements on our to-do lists or daily calendars. This is why such things as prayer can feel passé. It is a sense of meaning and mission that transforms prayer from being a domestic intercom into a wartime walkie-talkie—in other words, prayer infused with purpose. Many of us need to look in the mirror and ask the hard questions: What am I doing here? What do I live for? We need to regain a mission in life. We need to cultivate meaning.

Holy Closed-Mindedness

A possible subset of this problem is a growing unwillingness or inability to hold convictions, especially unpopular ones. A dominant virtue among younger people today is openness. There's nothing worse to some than being labeled a zealot or fundamentalist. The idea of being closed-minded is repugnant. Often, the goal is to be "balanced" and well-rounded—in a word, cultured. One writer speaks of the "openness of indifference," which is a kind of open-mindedness that looks as if it's acting on principle but is often just driven by what's fashionable.[26] I see this posture in theological, political, or other potentially contentious conversations. I also see it displayed in the dizzying array of "interests" people claim to have. We want to be eclectic, even eccentric. No one wants to be put in a box. Yet, what we have with "openness" is just a sophisticated version of "fear of man." We don't want to come off the wrong way or offend others with our convictions. But what ends up happening is that we lose our edge; we lose what should drive our actions—conviction and sense of purpose. We become jellyfish.

We have to ask ourselves: If everything is equally true or every perspective is equally valid, why bother caring about my own view? Why bother caring about anything? Unfettered open-mindedness is a bedfellow of apathy. It erodes conviction.

So, I want to advocate for what I call a "holy closed-mindedness"— which is just a way of saying "conviction." Part of what it might look like to cultivate meaning is to develop a kind of closed-mindedness, a willingness to be about something. It's really hard to hold a life-unifying sense of mission if I'm unwilling to be defined by anything.

So, what are some ways to cultivate meaning?

Practices for Cultivating Meaning

1. *Get clear on your convictions and values.* What are some things that you're certain about regarding your faith, the world, the Lord? What are the nonnegotiables of your life? Are they values such as hospitality, the desire to make an impact, a willingness to be a servant, authenticity? How would you like to be remembered?

26 Allan Bloom, *The Closing of the American Mind* (New York: Touchstone, 1988), 40–41.

Make a list of the things about which you will not budge regarding how your life is oriented or directed. Revisit that list periodically. Sometimes a loss of meaning in your life is just that—a loss. You once may have had a clearer sense of what you were about, but it somehow got pushed out of your mind and heart. Reclaim it by reminding yourself before the Lord of who you are, what you value, and what you want to be characteristic of your life. If you're at a loss about your convictions, you have some rich fodder for prayer and study.

2. *Take silence seriously.* Author Cal Newport argues that we as a Western society are suffering from "solitude deprivation," which is a "state in which you spend close to zero time alone with your own thoughts and free from input from other minds."[27] We are deluged with content—some trivial, some meaningful, but all of it ever-present. We have to make planned solitude a priority. How else can we have the space to process our thoughts, our feelings, our sense of calling, our values, our mission? We know it was the regular practice of our Lord to steal away for times of solitude and prayer (Matt. 14:13, 23; Luke 4:1–2; 5:16; 6:12). Jesus took time to prepare for difficult days ahead, to grieve, and to pray deeply. I'm convinced we can't even pray well unless we're clear on what's going on inside us. For that to happen, we need space. Now, we can take silence and solitude seriously in at least two ways: as major events or as mini-breaks. First, we can plan times of extended solitude (maybe twenty-four hours) when we go away somewhere and get off the grid. Second—and I think this may be more helpful for most—we can insert moments of

27 Cal Newport, *Digital Minimalism: Choosing a Focused Life in a Noisy World* (New York: Portfolio/Penguin, 2019), 103.

solitude into our everyday lives. Newport suggests, quite helpfully, that we make a practice of leaving our phones at home once in a while. We can also choose to not listen to a podcast or anything else on our fifteen-minute drive to work or thirty-minute run. Small choices like these can help declutter our minds, freeing us to think about what really matters.

3. *Take Sabbath even more seriously.* Our productivity does not define us. An overfocus on work causes us to lose perspective. We think, "Only what I do matters! Work is my reason for being!" These are lies that end up stripping us of meaning in our lives. Sabbath allows us to emotionally and mentally step back and put things in their proper perspective. Set a day when you rest those parts of yourself that are most deeply engaged in the six-day-a-week grind. Rest your body and mind. Be refreshed by personal and corporate worship, relationships, a hobby, reading, and times of prayerful reflection.

4. *Embrace "slow" and long-form media.* If you skate on the surface of life, it's difficult to develop conviction and a sense of meaning. If all you digest are sound bites by the dozen, you can be deceived into thinking you have deep feelings about a range of issues, when in fact your thoughts and feelings are a hundred miles wide and half an inch deep. Closely related to the need for solitude is the need to slow down in your intake of information, news, media, and so forth. One way to fend off the onslaught of the trivial is to commit yourself to reading longer, more thoughtful pieces of writing rather than five hundred-word, cobbled-together "news" articles (let alone 280-character tweets). The recent "Slow Media" movement in Europe developed largely to combat the thinning out of thoughtful and meaningful media. One point

of its "Manifesto" declares, "Slow media promote Monotasking. Slow Media cannot be consumed casually, but provoke the full concentration of their users. . . . Slow Media can only be consumed with pleasure in focused alertness."[28] Allow yourself to track with an argument from start to finish. Allow yourself to think deeply. In other words, make a point of limiting fast-food media consumption. It is all empty calories and doesn't contribute to a thoughtful and grounded life. One good essay or good book is worth a hundred headlines and tweets.

5. *Practice gratitude.* It is surprising how much thankfulness pervades the New Testament. Everywhere we look, someone is giving thanks or exhorting us to abound in thanksgiving. Paul sees the refusal to give thanks to God as at the core of human rottenness (Rom. 1:21). He makes the increasing of thankfulness to God one of his chief ministry objectives (2 Cor. 4:15; 9:11–12). He instructs us that everything we do should be done with thankfulness to the Father (Col. 3:17) because that is a summary of God's will for us (1 Thess. 5:18). But gratitude is also subversive. Paul says in Ephesians 5:4, "Let there be no filthiness nor foolish talk nor crude joking, which are out of place, but instead let there be thanksgiving." Notice that thanksgiving is that which replaces or, better, undermines filthy, vain, trivial, and mocking talk. We replace triviality with gratitude to God. Calling out all the good things we have from God immediately gives perspective to our daily lives. Paul even implies that the practice of giving thanks infuses meaning to every good gift God has given: "Nothing is to be rejected if it is received with thanksgiving" (1 Tim. 4:4).

28 "The Slow Media Manifesto," Slow Media, http://en.slow-media.net/. I draw this point from Newport, *Digital Minimalism*, 236–49.

Start small by thanking God every morning for everyday things, such as a warm shower, breakfast, your family, a job to go to, a car to take you to work, and more. Make it a habit to begin your day with thankfulness. During tough seasons, pause and write down things for which you're thankful. Figure out how to make gratitude a regular feature of your life. It will bring focus to your life if you will allow it to become a habit.

Cultivate Sacrificial Generosity

How do we arrive at the good life? Is it by accumulating as much as we can? No. Instead, the biblical response is radically counter-cultural: give your life away. For those who know Jesus Christ, sacrificial generosity arises from receiving God's generosity.

The apostle Paul, in 2 Corinthians 8–9, expends a great deal of ink spelling out the connection between God's generosity and our own. On the one hand, God's grace should motivate generosity: "For you know the grace of our Lord Jesus Christ, that though he was rich, yet for your sake he became poor, so that you by his poverty might become rich" (2 Cor. 8:9). Yet, equally striking, Paul declares how God "loves a cheerful giver" (9:7), blessing the generous giver more than the skimpy one (v. 6). Being generous allows us to experience God's grace in fresh ways as we participate in his generosity.

What does sacrificial generosity look like? C. S. Lewis offers some counsel:

I do not believe one can settle how much we ought to give. I am afraid the only safe rule is to give more than we can spare. In other words, if our expenditure on comforts, luxuries, amusements, etc., is up to the standard common among those with the same income as our own, we are probably giving away too little. If our charities do not at all pinch or hamper us, I should say they are too small. There ought to be things we should like to do and cannot do because our charities expenditure excludes them.[29]

True generosity pinches; it hurts. But it's not all pain and pinch that we're setting ourselves up for. "Whoever sows sparingly will also reap sparingly, and whoever sows bountifully will also reap bountifully" (2 Cor. 9:6). Blessing comes to those who willingly give generously. This principle is captured in a riddle posed by Mr. Honest to Gaius in John Bunyan's *The Pilgrim's Progress*:

A man there was, tho' some did count him mad
the more he cast away, the more he had.

Gaius, who fancies a good mystery, ponders the riddle and interprets it:

He that bestows his Goods upon the Poor
Shall have as much again, and ten times more.

Gaius explains that his ability to understand the riddle comes from his personal experience of this truth.[30] Then he quotes Proverbs 11:24:

One gives freely, yet grows all the richer;
another withholds what he should give, and only suffers want.

29 Lewis, *Mere Christianity*, 78.
30 John Bunyan, *The Pilgrim's Progress* (Ware: Wordsworth, 1996), 215–16.

John D. Rockefeller, the billionaire businessman and philan-
thropist, believed that God gave him the ability to attain great
wealth so that he could use it to benefit others. He held that if he
didn't share his wealth wisely and generously, God would take it
away. However, he—like Gaius—also believed that being generous would result in greater wealth to the giver. Thus, he lavishly
gave of his fortune to found institutions such as the University of
Chicago and Spelman College, and to support countless causes,
from foreign missions to public health.[31]

Research on charitable giving confirms this truth. Economist
Arthur Brooks observes that not only does giving increase with
increased income, but the opposite occurs: income increases as
giving increases. In 2000, every dollar donated to charity was associated with $4.35 in increased income. The data shows that the
charitable person earns about $14,000 more than the uncharitable
person. Equally astounding is the connection between individual
charity and the wealth of the nation. Brooks makes the point that
if individual charitable donations in the United States were cut
in half—a $95 billion loss—this would lead to an overall $1.8
trillion decline in national income.[32] The main point here (beyond
the technical economic stuff) is that giving has a "spillover effect"
much larger than the specific dollars given. Giving multiplies
wealth, and a lack of giving reduces potential wealth, both on an
individual and a national level.

Yet, it's not the financial benefits of generosity that I'm mainly
concerned with here. Brooks also points to noneconomic benefits

---

31 Arthur C. Brooks, *Who Really Cares: The Surprising Truth about Compassionate Con-
servatism* (New York: Basic, 2006), 137–40.

32 Brooks, *Who Really Cares*, 148.

of giving. For example, charity transforms givers, helping them become more humane. Charity also provides a sense of meaning by orienting life around a purpose outside ourselves. One survey of Americans shows that those who give money to charity are 43 percent more likely to say they are "very happy" than nongivers. In fact, nongivers are three and a half times more likely than givers to say they are "not happy at all." Givers are 25 percent more likely than nongivers to say that their health is excellent or very good, while nongivers are twice as likely to say that their health is poor or fair. There are similar results in the cases of volunteering and blood donation. For instance, elderly people who volunteer are 40 percent less likely to die in a given year than nonvolunteers of the same age and health level. Unsurprisingly from a Christian point of view, researchers have also found that formal volunteering causes significant improvements to mental health, resulting in the volunteers benefiting more than those they are helping. Even issues such as depression are lessened by volunteering.[33] And those who make a practice of being generous benefit far more than those who only sporadically display generosity.[34] Giving makes us happier and healthier people. In biblical categories, those willing to lose their life will gain it (see Luke 9:24).

Scripture and the social scientific research that agrees with it should compel us to ask how generosity might help alleviate the malaise of apathy. One link is found in the connection between giving and meaning. Apathy doesn't thrive in a meaning-filled environment. Generosity of time and money leads to a greater

33 See Brooks, *Who Really Cares*, 140–53.
34 Christian Smith and Hilary Davidson, *The Paradox of Generosity: Giving We Receive, Grasping We Lose* (New York: Oxford University Press, 2014), 29.

sense of purpose and meaning. It cuts through the trivial and brings us face-to-face with the real needs of the world. Generosity also turns our attention away from our griefs, our insecurities, and our fears—some of the other debilitating causes of apathy—and toward others. Yet, above all else, God gives grace to the giver. Willard is right when he says, "Our need to give is greater than God's need to receive. . . . But how nourishing to our faith are the tokens of God's care in response to our sacrifice."[35] So, to combat apathy, we must cultivate generosity.

However, we must be careful not to see generosity as merely a means to an end. Generosity is love in action. It should be a defining characteristic of the Christian. Even without the other benefits, generosity is a good thing in itself (in fact, we might lose its benefits if we practice generosity only for those other reasons).

What are some practices that will help foster generosity?

Practices for Cultivating Generosity

1. *Give away your time.* For many of us, time is our most precious commodity. We are tempted to be stingy with it. That means that cultivating sacrificial generosity means releasing our grip on our time.

There are countless practices by which you can give away your time. For example:

- *Commit to areas of regular service both within and outside of the church.* Be realistic about how much time you can devote, but be committed. Serving the body of Christ is a biblical

---

35 Willard, *Spirit of the Disciplines*, 175.

priority that results in a spiritual harvest for the server (Gal. 6:9–10). Serving outside of the church will expand your world and may put you in contact with different kinds of people, which can help jolt you out of your slumber.

- *Show hospitality to strangers.* Commit to sharing a monthly (or every other month) meal with someone from outside your circle of friends. Make the decision to invite someone new to your table six to twelve times a year. Hospitality does not need to be extravagant, only sincere.

2. *Give away your attention.* Even when we're with people, we can sometimes be present in body but absent in spirit. Time is not the only commodity we horde. We also withhold our attention from others. We are also prone to be quick to speak and slow to listen, even in friendly conversations.

How might you combat these tendencies and cultivate a generosity of attention?

- *Set aside one conversation per week in which you simply listen and ask genuine follow-up questions.* Then, after the conversation, make sure to follow up with the person.
- *Put away and silence your phone.* Phones are the ultimate attention divider. Unless you're expecting an important call or text, make it a habit to put your phone out of sight and even silence it during longer conversations with family members, friends, or coworkers.

3. *Give away your money.* The focus of this section has been on money, and rightly so. Jesus sees money as a (maybe even *the*)

chief competitor to his lordship in our lives. Our money often goes wherever our hearts are, and vice versa. We must be actively engaged in dethroning mammon, and this involves integrating some practices into our everyday lives.

Try one or two of the following:

- *Fast from Amazon.* For one week a month, avoid going to your favorite shopping site (for me, it's Amazon). This will help train your heart to think less in terms of buying, consuming, and accumulating. The omnipresence of internet shopping fosters a greater temptation than ever before to shop (or browse) as a pastime. If you want to be generous, you have to fight against being a perpetual consumer.

- *Prioritize regular giving.* Sporadic generosity is often less helpful to both the giver and the recipient. Regular giving will force you to give not just when you feel like it or are excited, but even when it pinches. Ministries count on and plan in light of regular giving. If giving in an automated way tends to distance your heart from the giving, then commit to giving online or by check (or even cash!) each month. Give to your church as a priority (Gal. 6:6) and to other causes that light your fire.

- *Take a "ninety-day giving challenge."* A friend of mine encourages people to pray and ask the Lord what he would have them give to their churches over the course of a three-month period. Drawing on 2 Corinthians 8–9, he gives them a ninety-day challenge of giving bountifully rather than sparingly—whether out of their poverty or wealth.[36]

36 John Rinehart, *Giving Together: An Adventure in Generosity* (Fullerton: Reclaimed, 2018), 66–69.

If done every three months, this could be one possible way for you to keep your giving both regular and attuned to the Spirit's direction.

Cultivate Fortitude

Those committed to fighting apathy must resolve to grow in emotional and spiritual toughness—that is, they must cultivate fortitude. We need to develop the kind of endurance and perseverance in hardship that counters the reflex to flee difficulty. Avoiding pain doesn't only weaken us, it eventually numbs us to all the possible pain-causing yet meaningful things we may be called to engage.

Remember the logic of Romans 5:3–4: "We rejoice in our sufferings, knowing that suffering produces endurance, and endurance produces character, and character produces hope." This process doesn't happen automatically. In fact, we could imagine a quite opposite process: suffering produces pulling away, which produces fragility, which leads to fear, which leads to pulling away (and the cycle repeats itself). However, the faith-filled person can face suffering head-on because he knows that suffering has a payoff. It produces endurance, which produces proven character, which then results in hope—the hope that we will not ultimately be swallowed up by our hardships. Seeing God protect and refine us through suffering then generates greater hope and trust that God will continue to carry us to our ultimate destination—to be like Christ and to be with Christ.[37] And then the cycle begins again: hope leads to perseverance, and so forth. Now, recall that

37 See Thomas R. Schreiner, *Romans*, Baker Exegetical Commentary on the New Testament (Grand Rapids, MI: Baker Academic, 2005), 256.

hopelessness is a major contributor to apathy. Yet, ironically, a sure path to hope is affliction. Therefore, embracing suffering is the way to spiritual vitality and strength. The only way up is through.

Opportunities to cultivate fortitude are sometimes less obvious and less dramatic than the term *suffering* connotes. Consider a 2013 ad for Facebook Home called "Family Dinner." During a family meal, a certain relative drones on and on about the wonders of finding the pet aisle at the grocery store. But one young woman refuses to endure the boredom. Instead, she swipes through her Facebook Home app, immersing herself in the world of her friends' posts, completely avoiding the uncomfortable and all-too-common family situation. Shannon Vallor, in her book *Technology and the Virtues*, draws attention to this ad and asks, What might this young woman have done if using Facebook at a family dinner had simply been out of bounds? Vallor's response: "She might have mustered the courage to interrupt and change the subject. She might have engaged in sympathetic eye-rolling with a fellow family hostage across the table. She might have started a quiet side conversation. She might have just sucked it up and patiently waited it out."[38] In other words, by escaping to Facebook Land and avoiding the uncomfortable, the young woman missed the opportunity to display and develop virtues such as courage, empathy, forbearance, fortitude, and patience. You see, virtues develop by practice, not by simply hoping they'll magically appear. As I've said before, we become what we do. If I disengage, I become disengaged. The more difficulty I avoid, the smaller (and deader) my heart becomes.

---

38 Shannon Vallor, *Technology and the Virtues: A Philosophical Guide to a Future Worth Wanting* (New York: Oxford University Press, 2016), 162.

The monk Evagrius of Pontus connects acedia (something like apathy) to perseverance. He counsels fellow monks,

> You must not abandon the cell in the time of temptations, fashioning excuses seemingly reasonable. Rather, you must remain seated inside, exercise perseverance, and valiantly welcome all attackers, especially the demon of acedia, who is the most oppressive of all but leaves the soul proven to the highest degree. Fleeing and circumventing such struggles teaches the mind to be unskilled, cowardly, and evasive.[39]

We may not be monks living in small cells, but God places us in situations that we are often tempted to flee. Evagrius's counsel is to not run from the things we find difficult or to try and distract ourselves out of apathy by filling our lives with painless trifles. Rather, we should embrace hardship, accept the difficult situations, face head-on the tasks we're called to, and persevere in hope that, as we stay faithful to our callings, God will produce fruit—even enabling us to overcome apathy itself. "Perseverance," writes Evagrius, "is the severing of acedia."[40]

In fact, I'm inclined to think that suffering is the very thing God often ordains to free us from apathy. Yet, it is the very thing we avoid, so we end up aiding and abetting the thing we're trying to defeat. Bearing a cross is an ordinary part of the Christian's life. The cross of hardship is actually a feature of God's fatherly care for us. John Calvin speaks of suffering as medicine, through which God

---

39 *Evagrius of Pontus: The Greek Ascetic Corpus*, trans. Robert E. Sinkewicz, Oxford Early Christian Studies (Oxford: Oxford University Press, 2003), 102.
40 *Evagrius of Pontus*, 64.

"confronts us and subjects and restrains our unrestrained flesh with the remedy of the cross."[41] When we become complacent and tepid in our spiritual lives, God sometimes confronts us with hardship as a means of waking us up. As Lewis so famously put it, "God whispers to us in our pleasures, speaks in our conscience, but shouts in our pain: it is His megaphone to rouse a deaf world."[42] This is why the psalmist can sing, "It is good for me that I was afflicted, / that I might learn your statutes" (Ps. 119:71). The "learning" here isn't academic. Learning is about truly knowing, revering, treasuring, and loving. Affliction taught the psalmist to commit himself more fully to God's word. Hardship—God's megaphone—moved him from stubbornness and indifference to wholehearted commitment to God.

How, then, might we cultivate strength, perseverance, and fortitude?

Practices for Cultivating Fortitude

1. *Feed faith and hope, not the opposite.* "One must train the habit of Faith," Lewis says.[43] If you are particularly prone to doubt or despair, or find yourself fearful about hardship, one of the most foundational things you can do is build up faith and hope through the promises of Scripture. Focus on passages that remind you of (1) who God is, (2) his presence in your suffering, (3) what he is doing through your suffering, and (4) the Christian's ultimate

---

41 John Calvin, *Institutes of the Christian Religion*, ed. John T. McNeill, trans. Ford Lewis Battles, The Library of Christian Classics, vols. 20–21 (Philadelphia: Westminster, 1960), 3.8.5, 706.

42 C. S. Lewis, *The Problem of Pain* (Glasgow: Collins, 1987), 74.

43 Lewis, *Mere Christianity*, 122.

hope of being with and like Christ. Also, find models among those who have suffered well, even while never having their difficulties removed by God. Read their biographies as part of your regular spiritual diet. Learn their secrets. Be ruthless about lowering the volume on influences that communicate that this world is all we have. Turn up the volume on those voices that encourage you toward Christian hope. And pray, pray, pray for faith.

2. *Process grief, disappointment, and doubt.* Grief is a response to pain, suffering, and loss. When left unprocessed, it can have ever-increasing and ever-surprising effects on your soul, such as nurturing depression and apathy. You need to confront your grief. It may be a worthwhile investment to pursue professional counseling as one way to address grief. Weekly engagement with a counselor will force you to not avoid pain, but to pass through the pain to healing. If doubt is the issue, work through whether your doubts are intellectual or emotional, and then confront them head-on.

3. *Choose to talk about Jesus.* I wanted to entitle this practice "Share your faith." But I've found over the years that when Christians are told to share their faith, they feel as if it's too big an ask. One reason is that they find it difficult to talk about Jesus even among fellow Christians. There's a fear of being dismissed as superspiritual or, if you're among intellectuals, of being seen as simple. No matter the reason, boldness to talk about Jesus welcomes ridicule or disrespect—in a word, hardship. However, you want to press into that hardship rather than avoid it. So, one potential way to cultivate fortitude is to try and talk about Jesus—something about your actual relationship with him—with someone you don't typically talk with on that level. Make it your

aim to do this once a week or once a month. It doesn't need to be a nonbeliever or a stranger. But try to embrace the discomfort. We develop strength by exercising our muscles. We foster courage by entering the fray. Take baby steps if necessary. Who knows, you may find yourself growing increasingly passionate about your own faith and bold about sharing it with nonbelievers as a result.

4. *Finish stuff.* While I'm not one who believes you have to read every book from start to finish, I'm aware that never finishing anything I start is a poor habit to fall into. Make a list of unfinished projects, unresolved items on your to-do list, or half-read books on your nightstand. Plan to finish one of these items every week or month (or in whatever time frame is suitable). Persevering in the small things enlarges our capacity to endure bigger things.

Fight the Good Fight

We are not destined to a life of apathy. We are Christians, not fatalists. Yet, there is no silver bullet when it comes to slaying apathy in our lives. I'm sure that's obvious to anyone who's struggled with it. Neither is there a seven-step plan—but that doesn't mean there is no strategy whatsoever. As Bunyan writes, God has placed "steps" in the midst of our "slough of despond," even if we often fail to take those steps. The strategy I've proposed in this chapter is that of cultivating certain postures by adopting particular practices in our lives. These are some of the "steps" I think God provides to help us through the mire of apathy.

I'm aware that talking about apathy as sin and recommending things to do about it can sound dour, pessimistic, and even legalistic to some. Yet, I'm convinced that legalism is the least of our worries. Piper puts it this way:

> The creeping legalism in American evangelicalism today, I believe, is not the spiritual discipline of Daniel who prayed three times a day. I urge you to consider whether some of our weakness rather in cushy, self-indulgent, so-called spontaneous, meet-my-needs, American Christianity is owing not mainly to bondage to legalistic lists of dos and don'ts, but rather to the fact that we have forsaken biblical discipline.[44]

We can grab hold of our spiritual lives and discipline ourselves through practices like these. Yes, I could have suggested more practices or disciplines and could have said more things, since what we're really talking about is the grand matter of how to form spiritually vibrant people. There are millennia of wisdom on that topic—too much for one chapter of a very short book. But at the very least, these practices are a start, even though I think they're more than that. They are some of the Spirit's weapons in the fight to suppress the meh and sustain zeal for God. Paul exhorts Timothy, "Fight the good fight of the faith," which is shorthand for what he instructs right before that: "Pursue righteousness, godliness, faith, love, steadfastness, gentleness" (1 Tim. 6:11–12). We fight the good fight *by* pursuing these virtues. And we pursue these virtues by finding concrete ways to practice and develop them in the day-to-day.

---

44 John Piper, "Consistent Spiritual Discipline Is Not Legalism," *Ask Pastor John* podcast, episode 701, October 7, 2015, Desiring God, https://www.desiringgod.org/.

Fight the good fight against apathy. Combat through cultivation. Change is possible, but there are no shortcuts.[45]

Let me build, then, my King,
a beautiful thing by long obedience,
by the steady progression of small choices
that laid end to end will become like the stones
of a pleasing path stretching to eternity and
unto your welcoming arms and unto the sound
of your voice pronouncing the judgment:

Well done.

Questions for Reflection

1. How do you respond to the idea of cultivating virtues as a key way to combat apathy? Does this strike you as motivating? Discouraging?

2. Identify one or two practices that you can realistically see yourself starting. What might be some obstacles that might hinder you from gaining momentum in those areas? What can you do to prevent those potential obstacles from tripping you up?

---

45 The following prayer is taken from Douglas Kaine McKelvey, *Every Moment Holy*, vol. 1 (Nashville: Rabbit Room, 2017), 163.

Concluding Thoughts

WHEN YOU COME TO the end of a book you're reading, it's common to wish this or that had been said or a certain topic had been developed more. There will undoubtedly be itches that weren't scratched and subtleties that were left unaddressed in this book. As I said at the outset, I make no claim to being comprehensive or definitive in my reflections on apathy. Yet, there are a few matters that didn't fit neatly into the flow of the chapters that I'd like to speak to as we draw this book to a close. I present them as four caveats to our discussion.

Caveat 1: Sin patterns in our lives may lead to spiritual coldness. A possible cause of spiritual blahness is an ongoing choice to walk in sinful disobedience to God in some area of life unrelated to apathy. If we are unremorseful or unrepentant about these sins, we may find ourselves feeling cold, distant, and disinterested. This experience *may* be God allowing our fellowship with him to cool as a way of snapping us out of our sinful stupor and drawing us to him in repentance. This caveat can be easily misunderstood. I'm not saying that if someone struggles with a particular sin, God will punish him or her with apathy. I am speaking about the *possibility* that unconfessed and willful sin will blunt our passion. We often misuse the word *struggle*, adopting it to describe our regular giving in to sin without a fight rather than our conscious and active battle against it (which we *do* sometimes lose). Instead of fighting, we indulge the sin. This isn't struggle, it's surrender. If we are regularly surrendering to sin, we shouldn't be surprised if apathy follows. But like the writer of Hebrews, I "feel sure of better things" (Heb. 6:9) for readers of this book.

Caveat 2: You may feel apathetic, but apathy is not really the issue. As I mentioned in chapter 2, apathy may be a symptom of something else. Depression is a common cloak for apathy. It is often the main issue to which our apathy is pointing. We need to ask ourselves (or others) if we are depressed. If we are, then we should pursue counseling as a way to process our depression and work toward wholeness. Apathy will likely fade if we deal with the real issues surrounding depression. However, if we are apathetic but not depressed, we must still do the work of trying to understand why. I've offered seven possible causes; there could be many more. Once we've discerned the probable causes, we can then think about the kinds of remedies that will address them. Whether processing the depression that expresses itself as apathy, or processing apathy itself, the path of overcoming is a lengthy one. It may take weeks, months, or longer, but that may be part of what it means to "work out your own salvation with fear and trembling" (Phil. 2:12).

Caveat 3: Passion can look different at different ages. There is a thing called "youthful zeal," which can be a good thing. But youthful zeal will typically be chastened by time and life experiences. For example, my zeal for my marriage is deeper today than it was on my wedding day, and I often express that zeal quietly and consistently, but perhaps without the same fanfare I might have in the early days. Perhaps passion for God works similarly. The way I expressed love for him in my twenties differs in some respects from the way I express it in my forties. This is not to say there aren't important overlaps—Jesus does call the church back to the way it loved him at first (Rev. 2:4–5). But passion takes different forms at different life stages. Energy levels decline, mobility decreases, and we become more even-tempered, more measured. Yet, our resolute devotion to the Lord and to loving others with our actions should not wane. I say this so that fifty-somethings do not feel pressure to respond to God like teenagers at youth camp.

Caveat 4: Different personality types or temperaments may express passion differently. I hesitate to include this as a caveat because I know it can easily be used as an excuse for lack of zeal for God (I probably have similar hesitations over the previous caveat). Yet, it would be unwise to ignore the fact that people of similar ages may express zeal in diverse ways. Some people are more effusive in their passion, while others are quiet and calm. Both are equally passionate, but the optics are different. And we may too quickly label the one zealous and the other cold. We must, therefore, allow for variety in expressions of zeal. A good diagnostic question for the quietly zealous might be this: Is there anything that elicits expressive praise from me? For instance, if I view myself as having a quiet temperament, but am easily jazzed about Manchester United or find myself able to cheer at a Buffalo Bills touchdown—is it really a temperament issue? Make room for temperament, but don't make temperament an escape clause.

To the sinful, depressed, aged, and reserved—God knows your frame. He accepts no excuses, but extends abundant grace. And to all of us, as we draw these reflections to a close: "Do not be slothful in zeal, be fervent in spirit, serve the Lord" (Rom. 12:11).

Acknowledgments

I HAVE REGULARLY EXPERIENCED the reality that book writing is a community effort. I'm thankful for the many people who contributed to this book.

Thanks to Ken Berding for numerous conversations during walks around Creek Park, for encouragement, for careful feedback, and for countless ideas—some of which he didn't realize he was giving.

I'm grateful to Kyle Lundquist for providing insights and asking key questions that helped me initially frame the book, as well as offering gracious feedback on the chapters.

Thanks to Jeremy Lupinacci for consistently prodding me to go ahead and write this book, and for thoughtful notes on my chapters.

I'm grateful to Hank Voss for help thinking through the structure of the book, feedback, and helpful resources along the way.

Thanks to Ryan Schuler and Nick Kaschuk for reading through two key chapters and providing extensive feedback.

Kyle Strobel, Jordan Barrett, Greg Peters, and Steve Pardue connected me with valuable resources.

I'm grateful as always to Talbot School of Theology for a research leave that freed me up to work on this project (particularly during the challenging early days of COVID-19) and to Biola University for providing a generous research grant that helped fund my leave.

Samuel James, Greg Bailey, and the Crossway team have been a joy to work with. Many thanks for taking on this project with enthusiasm.

Finally, as always, I'm most thankful to my wife, Melissa—for her support and for long nights of carefully reading through my manuscript and offering insightful comments on every chapter— and to my kids, Zoe, Eli, and Ezra. May we all live each day free from the curse of apathy and with ever-increasing zeal for God.

General Index

love, 45, 129, 142
Lukianoff, Greg, 90
Luther, Martin, 90, 111–12

Macdonald, George, 69
Macintyre, Ben, 42
MAD TV, 141–42
Manning, Brennan, 146
Married with Children, 21
Mary Magdalene, 106–7
Matheson, George, 97–100
maturity, 61, 88
McLuhan, Marshall, 80
meaning, 147–55
meaninglessness, 73, 118
mental health, 72, 158
mindset, 87
mission, 28, 147–55
monasticism, 62
money, 160–61
moods, 71
moral accountability, 25
motivation, 52, 54, 56, 76
mystery, 69

new creation, 102
Newport, Cal, 152–53
new spirit, 149–50
Nietzsche, Friedrich, 73, 90
nihilism, 84–85, 118
"ninety-day giving challenge,"
    161–62
nonpassivity, 35
nuance, 36
numbness, 75, 83

obsessive–compulsive symptoms,
    72
"O Love That Wilt Not Let Me Go"
    (Matheson), 97–98
online games, 85–86

"on the spot," 133
openness, 150–51
Orwell, George, 79
outrage, 22

parable, 143–44
parable of the workmen, 110
paradox, 23, 37
paranoia, 72
Parkinson's disease, 52
passion, 17, 31–34, 43, 140, 143,
    172–73
pastoral theology, 12
patience, 67, 113–15
peace, 124–25
peanut allergies, 90
perseverance, 164
personality types, 173
perspective, 118–20
Peterson, Jordan, 84–85
Philby, Kim, 41–43
philosophical doubt, 70
philosophy, 43, 69
Phinehas, 32–33
phones, 160
Pilgrim's Progress, The, 59, 156
Piper, John, 93, 147, 168
plague, 32
Plantinga, Cornelius, 64
political reform, 121
pop culture, 21
Postman, Neil, 79–81
practical theology, 12
prayer, 27, 37–38
preaching, 17
Protestants, 29
psychological studies, 115
Puritans, 37
purpose, 83, 92–94
purposelessness, 51, 126–27

Scripture Index